Sociologist Seeking Justice:

A Grandfather's Guide to Discussing Whiteness, White Privilege, and White Supremacy

DWIGHT W. JACKSON, PhD

DEDICATION

My Family
Ancestors, you changed the story of those who came before you. Alec, Brittany, Ally, Justin, Kyla, Landon, Payton, Micah, Autumn, Aiden, Brooks, and Evan, do the same. .

CONTENTS

Introduction

When I have been asked why I write, I usually respond "I do it for myself." This is always true. In this text other motivations play a significant part.

The length of time that it has taken for me to become aware of the issues addressed in this text embarrasses me. Each reasoned explanation sounds like an excuse. The issues are important to me because they comprise much of who I am: person of faith, son, grandson, father, grandfather, and citizen. Seeing others similar to me struggle provides no comfort only greater embarrassment.

Several years ago, I was a member of the leadership team charged with establishing the Center for Community and Justice on my undergraduate campus. We failed. I learned much in the trying. The writings of John Powell, Steve Martinot, and Theodore Allen became important on the first reading. (there have been many since) Allen ties English activity in Ireland with the decisions in Jamestown which reminded me that my Morrison ancestor had passed through Ireland about the time of the Ulster Plantation. Research ties my Jackson ancestor there also. The history of racialization became personal.

The failure to launch the Center was personal too. People I respect opposed its establishment while supporting much of its intent. I wanted to make sense of this without dismissing them.

Whiteness and racialization are personal because of twelve important people, my grandchildren and great-grandson. They will come of age in a society that I know devalues half of them because they will not identify as white. I cannot change that. I do hope to contribute to the conversation.

ACKNOWLEDGMENTS

Ashley Jackson has taught me more lessons than she can imagine. Yohana Ndadabagome opened my eyes to the toll of discrimination. .Yves Habamugisha demonstrated the dignity that lives in those who have been abused. Linda Kessler showed me I should pay attention to the language I use. And my wife, Brenda, enabled the environment in which all these lessons were learned. Jessica and Edwin Estevez encouraged my academic perspective on the issues addressed in this book. Thanks to each and every one of you.

1 MOVING ON FROM MY FATHER'S HOUSE

> *Now the Lord said to Abram, "Go from your country and your kindred and your father's house to the land that I will show you. I will make of you a great nation, and I will bless you, and make your name great, so that you will be a blessing. (Gen. 12: 1-2) NRSV*

Being a white male in his late sixties puts me at a disadvantage for writing a book on racism in America. What I can do is speak to those (people like me) who have limited awareness that they create and maintain a system of racialization.

> [Racialization is} the set of practices, cultural norms, and institutional arrangements that both reflect and help to create and maintain race-based outcomes in society. Because racialization is a set of historical and cultural processes, it does not have one particular meaning. Instead, it describes conditions and norms that are constantly evolving and interacting with the sociopolitical environment, varying from location to location as well as throughout different periods of history.[1]

I will add a white family perspective to the discussion. Coming of age after the legislative gains in the 1960s, I was among those whites who considered the issue resolved. I was wrong. Being busy with living my

---

[1] Powell, (2012). p. 4

life was no excuse for indifference to the injustices of racism. I cannot defend the slow pace that marked the growth of what awareness and willingness for action that I now possess. My years of indifference, added to the indifference demonstrated by millions of others, created and maintains the system.

I was wrong because I accepted the assumptions of whiteness. I was wrong because I was unable to challenge those assumptions. I wasn't just wrong, I was unaware. Being unaware is the more shameful to me. I am the product of at least 13 generations of multiple family lineages participating in the construction and maintenance of race-based outcomes in our country. Depending upon the contributing line in my biography as many as 11 of those generations since coming to North America.

My ability to challenge these assumptions existed long before the challenging started. This same extended family passed to me values of fairness and a commitment to biblical authority. Understanding that I needed to apply these to the issues of whiteness and racism was the challenge. Formal and informal training developed a natural inclination to ask questions and seek reconciliation of those discrepancies with which I lived. Our adoption of an African-American daughter gave us a front row seat to the racism she experienced. We hurt with her in these experiences. As a father, I consider it a failure that I was unable to keep one of my children from being injured. Five of our eleven grandchildren are people of color. I am angry that the social world of which I am a member, which my family has maintained for more than eleven generations, will not treat them equally.

My father's house—metaphorically the place I must leave to gain the perspective and experience to live the life God intends. This is an important theme to this book. My father's house is a place in which I have learned whiteness. This is where I learned to tolerate acts of racialization. I finally heard the invitation and accepted the challenge of going to the context that is awaiting me in the land that God will show me.

In this book I will apply the perspective of my several areas of learning and training to evaluate this white perspective. I will, also, link the known members of my ancestral pool to the historical development of whiteness and racism in the United States. The purpose of this book is a demonstration that the production of whiteness in our society is a family occupation.

A Social Perspective

I am a sociologist. I am other things—husband, father, grandfather, businessman, Follower of Jesus, American—to name a few. As a sociologist, I teach concepts and application. I have taught in US universities and high schools, in university-level semester abroad programs in Thailand and Rwanda, and in pastor training programs in Kenya, Burundi, and Tanzania. My research focuses on non-profit organizations and the social aspects of communities with economic, political, and relational challenges. I find sociology to be a practical discipline.

Sociology is the study of human habits across space and time. As newborns, we enter the social world particularized by the habits of our parents and those with whom they associate. Before we can talk, we are exposed to these habits. Intentionally and unintentionally those who care for us shape our social identity by their habits. We imitate their habits, if we didn't social life would not be possible. In this way social life is structured by habits passed from one generation to the next. Over time the process of enacting our acquired habits will in fact alter those same habits.

While it is true that we enter a particularized social world, ours isn't the only one. All societies generally share patterns of habits. Language is such a habit. My social world regularly calls this item you are reading a book. My professional life has taken me to live in other social worlds where this is a *livre* or an *igitabo*. Language is a very useful habit and only one of the many that people need to share in order to constitute a society. We do not have time in this chapter to catalogue all of the habits we share in our particularized society. By the way, it is the habit of sociologists to refer to social habits as <u>institutions.</u>

I want my students to understand that our shared institutions make it possible for societies to create and distribute a wide range of social goods and services. Membership in the society is the most basic of all these goods. The more complicated and sophisticated the society the more elaborate the habits—rules, rituals, and interactions—associated with the level of membership or place in the society one occupies. Generally, a relative few members achieve a position of full membership in any given society. Varying levels of membership are distributed based on the characteristics identified, developed, valued, and habituated by that society.

These levels of membership are the basis for what sociologists refer to as <u>social stratification</u>. Various characteristics are used to create stratification. Among these are age, sex, gender, family, wealth, religion, profession, and race. If stratification, simply distributed social status across its membership than it would not merit all the attention we give it. Stratification is the distribution map of a society. Goods and services available in the society are unevenly distributed based on this map. Those levels considered "higher" demonstrate a greater concentration of power which enables members of these strata to tilt the "table" of their society in their favor by controlling access to goods and services. We will see how race in America acquired a role in the stratification map.

Sociology is found in the intersection of history and biography. My social facts are defined by this intersection. My family is Ozarkian from northern Arkansas, from a county my grandfather declared had never had a race problem. My mother editorialized that all blacks knew they should not be there after dark. My family came to Arkansas by way of Illinois, Tennessee, Kentucky, and Oklahoma. The generations before these came from Missouri, Georgia, North Carolina, Virginia, Maryland, and Pennsylvania. I grew up Southern Baptist, a denomination created to protect the right of slaveholders to be missionaries. As late as the

1960s no American people of color could be admitted to one of our colleges—yet we proudly related for all the world our education of Africans from our mission fields. Dad was a union carpenter.

From what my sister learned in her research into our family lines, our people farmed. With few exceptions they were yeomen farmers, growing what they consumed and trying to produce a small cash crop. We have some indication that they served in the military, as deputy sheriffs, as justices of the peace, stone quarry laborers, lumbermen, and skilled labor—electrician, plumber, and construction. Both my Jackson and Morrison ancestors entered the US by way of Pennsylvania. In the early years they were people of the frontier living in western North Carolina, Kentucky and Tennessee. The Carolinian Jacksons moved to northern Georgia around 1800 where my paternal great grandfather was born in 1845. He entered the Confederate Army at 15. Sometime between the end of the war and 1872 he moved to Howell County, Missouri. The maternal line of my family, the Morrisons, lived in Tennessee and Arkansas primarily. I will flesh out the time-line more fully when discussing the historic development of racism. My history and my biography were structured by institutions of racism. I find it unreasonable for me to deny that history and the foundational role it performed in shaping me for membership in US society.

Why do I place so much emphasis on this family biography? Socialization! Socialization is the term sociologists give this process of acquiring family habits, acquiring not having them imprinted. Socialization is an imperfect process. Children resist at some points, but by and large we share more family habits then we care to admit. Many family habits reside in our unconscious. We may never become aware of all our habits. Some like the racializing practices of my family only come to the surface over time and with the processing of personal contradictions.

Sociologist Anthony Giddens' structuration theory[2] is informative for explaining the racialization of my family. In his understanding, racism can only continue as an institution in American society to the extent that members reproduce it in pursuing social life. If we are acknowledged racists, then we are aware that we pursue racialized strategies. (Likely, a self-acknowledged racist never picked this book up or has put it down by now.) If you are unaware of the racialization patterns of your family, Giddens locates this process in the unacknowledged conditions of action for social agents (all of us).

As actors in social situations we exercise agency when we have the capability of alternative courses of action. That is good news for us. Our parents' habits are not deterministic. They do contribute to the unconscious portions of our personality. The presence of these patterns requires significant effort to detect. The unconscious houses those aspects of our history that are unavailable to us. We cannot acknowledge these conditions of action unless we can evaluate them. Along with the unconscious, practical consciousness contributes to the unacknowledged conditions of action. Generally practical consciousness can be explained but are not because we perform them without question.

The practical consciousness is the location for those habits that we utilize daily to reproduce our society as we pursue our goals. Most of these habits operate without our awareness. Think of it this way, if we had to be aware of all that we do in this area our brain would look like central Manhattan at rush hour. It is here that we find what we know about social conditions, particularly our social conditions but unless pushed we cannot put this knowledge into words. When pushed elements of the practical consciousness can be known in a discursive way.

---

[2] Giddens, (1984), p. 2-7

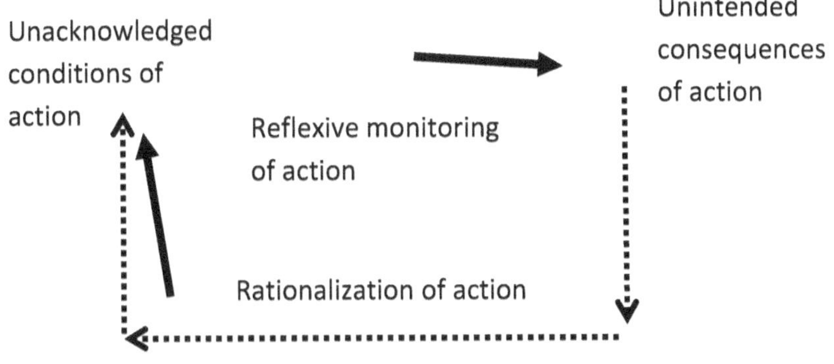

Gidden's Model for Agent Stratification of Action

The reflexive monitoring of action is our daily process to assess our action and the action of others. These actions are context specific. As competent social agents we learn how to operate within multiple contexts. We calculate the degree to which our action aligns with that of others. When our action achieves expected outcomes, the reflection is primarily comparison with the action of others and the willingness to change when we learn a better way. When unintended consequences occur then the agent is challenged to more carefully process their actions and its results. The rationalization of action is the capability by which we assure that our action makes sense and is consistent.

Some years ago, in St. Louis I was on a task force with the Jewish program director of Interfaith Partnership. We knew each other well enough to exchange small talk before and after meetings. One day we got to talking about my family's time in Africa. I was explaining bartering and how it worked in Burundi. In describing one situation I said, "After thirty minutes I was able to Jew him down to a third of his asking price." To which she said, "What did you say?" In that moment I realized that my family's use of this term did not fit this context. The unexpected challenge made me see this term through her eyes. The shift to discursive consciousness came as I was repeating the phrase 'Jew him down.' I have not used that phrase since except to relate this incident.

Oh by the way, this woman became a prime factor in Brenda and I adopting our last three children. So much so that she considered them her kids as well.

This book examines the intersection of my biography and history through my extended pool of ancestors as I examine one issue—whiteness. I will develop the argument that whiteness is a habit made possible by the rationalization of action and the unacknowledged conditions of action in the lives of agents which I assume is reflective of my larger family. From all accounts we are an all-American family. My ancestors (if you go back 10 generations there are 1,024 contributing lines) have worked hard, fought in wars (both sides of the Civil War), attended church, gone to prison, but we haven't found one slave owner. They may be there, we just haven't found them. What appears overwhelmingly true is that my 1,024 lines have lived in social spaces in which they were needed to perpetuate whiteness as a means to assure race-based outcomes.

I was raised in a context and a time (the 1960s) in which much of the practical knowledge that shaped my social formation could be challenged. The historical events of our society and my personal biography increased the likelihood that I would become more discursively aware of my racializing family influences. What has been less predictable is that my whiteness could be challenged. The acknowledgement of this condition has been more recent than my concern with racialization. I am convinced that I was among many whites who thought that we were helping to reduce racism. We did not understand that we were severely limited because we did not understand how it is constructed. Nor did we understand our role in perpetuating this habit.

Desegregation and the civil rights movement increased the amount of our societal racism that now is available to our collective discursive consciousness. If you doubt that racism still lingers in our collective unconsciousness and practical consciousness connect with those who remain the objects of its expressions. It has not been 15 years since my daughter and her friends were chased by 137 Caucasian students and some parents from Vandalia, IL. to the Value City parking lot on Old Highway 40 in Greenville, Il. The offense: attending a basketball game.

Desegregation and civil rights have exposed the conditions of whiteness. Why? I think that is because whiteness and its counterpart, racism, are family habits. A driving question of this book, "Can we change old destructive habits?" If so, will we?

Letting the Scriptures be Scripture

I was raised in a fundamentalist Southern Baptist Church that taught me to have a high regard for the authority of scriptures. That lesson persists to this day. Many of the particulars of my scriptural understandings have changed. The rationale they gave me is unsupportable, but the high regard remains. At the same time, I was encouraged by a strong, willed mother to think independently and to ask questions. And by her father who challenged me to seek the connections between what I observed when I paid attention to people.

In God's grace life experiences have challenged both my unacknowledged conditions of action and my rationalization of action. While attending Greenville College (now University) I encountered Drs. J.E. Hollister and James Reinhardt. Hollister built on the foundation laid by my mother and her father by adding a sociological framework. Reinhardt demonstrated that a man of faith could hold principles firmly with kindness and love.

In Africa, beginning with Danish and Barundi Baptists and Rwandan Free Methodists, I encountered faith frameworks nurtured in other cultural forms. These encounters challenged me to search scripture to square beliefs and practice different from those of my youth yet clearly effective in building the people of God. These experiences exposed the cultural basis for my rationalization of action, rationalizations that I had unreflectively assumed were biblical and not cultural and contextual.

An urban mission assignment took us with our four youngest children to

North St. Louis where we spent more than four years living in public housing. During that period, we observed the unequal distribution of social goods to people of color. The structural challenges of housing and the social network for poor African-Americans altered our perceptions of the challenges faced by the poor in our country, but particularly the poor who are also people of color.

In each of these situations the role of context or the role of a new context in challenging my rationalization of action is clear. What is less clear is the role scripture can play in creating a new context. One of the habits passed on to me, a high regard for scriptural authority, actually loops back for me in the reflexive nature that Giddens gives the 'knowledgeability' of agents. New contexts and understandings increased the likelihood that I would become aware of the contradictions of the claim in scripture on the actions and attitudes of the followers of Jesus and the degree to which my social actions fell short.

For thirty years, I was a pastor and missionary. Most of that ministry was in Africa and inner city St. Louis. Biblical studies and interpretation have been important to me. Recently I have been thinking and writing sociologically about the actions of Jesus to launch the Kingdom. Now I am turning to the same process for the early church. But I am stuck. I am stuck on the five statements Jesus made about the Holy Spirit and our lives in the Kingdom. In addition to comfort and convicting us of sin, the Spirit is to lead us into all truth. Does that process include the growth of our discursive consciousness? Does it impact the unacknowledged conditions for action? If so, is that process limited to individuals who are social agents? Does it include the habits we agents reproduce in our process of living in the world?

Let's listen to the Apostle Paul:

For we know that the law is spiritual; but I am of the flesh, sold into slavery under sin. I do not understand my own actions. For I do not do what I want, but I do the very thing I hate. Now if I do what I do not want, I agree that the law is good. But in fact it is no longer I that do it, but sin that dwells within me. For I know that nothing good dwells within me, that is, in my flesh. I can will what is right, but I cannot do it. For I do not do the good I want but the evil I do not want is what I do. Now if I do what I do not want, it is no longer I that do it, but sin that dwells within me.

So I find it to be a law that when I want to do what is good, evil lies close at hand. For I delight in the law of God in my inmost self, but I see in my members another law at war with the law of my mind, making me captive to the law of sin that dwells in my members. Wretched man that I am! Who will rescue me from this body of death? Thanks be to God through Jesus Christ our Lord. (Rom. 7:14-25a NRSV)

The law, the rules, "imply 'methodical procedure' of social action."[3] In this case they are the rules that Paul (and I) believe come with Divine authority. As rules they impact our understanding of what is meaningful and provide pressure to behave properly. For me this is greatly influenced by my understanding that my role as a Follower of Jesus is to reproduce the nature of the biblical God in my agency, in my social habits.

With Paul we must ask, "Who will deliver us from the habits of whiteness and acts of racialization?"

I appeal to you therefore, brothers and sisters, by the mercies of God, to present your bodies as a living

---

[3] Ibid p. 18

sacrifice, holy and acceptable to God, which is your spiritual worship. Do not be conformed to this world, but be transformed by the renewing of your minds, so that you may discern what is the will of God—what is good and acceptable and perfect. (Rom. 12:1-2 NRSV)

Transformed by the expansion of our Discursive Consciousness so that the healing presence of God can move us from acts of racialization—both in act and in unintended habit—to lives that build *Shalom*!

2 CREATING WHITENESS TO RIG THE SYSTEM

Socialization is the process through which a society stores its institutions and practical knowledge. While they are loving and nurturing us, our parents model these social facts within our consciousness. It is an unintended consequence of all that care. Parents exercise almost total dominance over infants and this dependency accentuates the effect of this transfer. In secondary socialization, teachers, coaches, and pastors, etc. have dominance—though less intense—over their charges. These 'authorities' model social knowledge within our consciousness. This is not a perfectly deterministic process. As any parent or teacher can affirm children have 'minds' of their own and will resist this imprinting process in a variety of ways. Socialization is sufficiently effective that social structures have passed from one generation to the next existed over millennia.

Our children grow up to join other actors in their society exercising their agency in pursuit of their purposes. Sociologist Anthony Giddens asserts, "Human societies, or social systems, would plainly not exist without human agency. But it is not the case that actors create social systems: they reproduce or transform them, remaking what is already made in the continuity of praxis".[4] Our children join a society, just as we did. As their socialization kicks in they join us in either reproducing or transforming our society.

---

[4] Giddens (1984), p. 171

The progression of history, whether that of my family or my country, is the story of generations being born into a social order, being socialized into that society, then pursuing their interests by means of the social skills they have learned. Thus, 'the continuity of praxis' becomes history. In this chapter we will explore 'the continuity praxis' that emerged with the development of English colonial practices in the Americas.

The history of my family is linked to and framed by the history of English colonialism in Ireland and in the United States. My sister Winona Matheson's family research is the foundation which I used to examine our family history. My quest to determine the proximity of ancestors to key events in the English timeline has revealed several points of contact. I use general information about these ancestors to place them within the flow of historical events.

Theodore Allen[5] provides the framework I use to interpret the historical context of my ancestors. By 1420 my line of Jacksons was in York, England. Six generations later, Anthony Jackson was a secretary to George Villiers and later became a Gentleman of the Privy Chamber of Charles I. His support of the Stuarts landed him in the Tower of London for eight years.

With the loss of their father's fortune, Anthony's three sons went to Ireland in 1648 as members of Cromwell's army. A year later they were granted manor estates from land confiscated from the Irish tribes. One of these was my 9x great grandfather, Richard. Around 1654 he was among a group of seven who were 'convinced' by the preaching of William Edmundson to form the first group of converts to the religious teachings of George Fox, Quakerism. Richard oriented his life to the launching of these teachings among the English in Ireland. Accounts of his changing places of residence coincide with the progression of the evangelistic effort. Richard spent at least one year in an Irish jail because of his evangelism work.

---

[5] Allen (1994)

Richard's grandson Thomas was born 21 June 1692 in Killenard, County Laois, Ireland. He was among the English Quakers who would migrate from Ireland to Pennsylvania. He died in 1727 and is buried in the New Garden Friends' Cemetery in Chester County, Pennsylvania. Myers[6] research supports the pattern of avoidance typical of English presence in Ireland. His work uncovered only three Irish surnames in the list of Quaker immigrants of this period.

My Mother's paternal line, the Morrisons, arrived in Ireland sometime after 1677. Her 5x great grandfather, John Morrison was born in 1677 at Isle Lewis, Hebrides, Scotland, moved to Ireland and was buried in Ulster in 1739. His son Samuel Morrison was born in Stewartstown, Tyrone, Northern Ireland in 1701, which places John in the middle of the plantation efforts of the English in the late 17th century. Isle Lewis is a rather remote and barren island. Scotland endured a famine in the 1690s. At the same time the English began importing Scottish to work the land in Tyrone area.

Samuel would immigrate to North America before 1756. Family legend identifies him as the founder of our American line and as a 'horse thief who escaped the sheriff by hiding in an empty whisky barrel just before it was loaded on a ship bound for North America.' Granted the story has issues, but what legend doesn't. The Morrisons originated in Scotland and never let anything get in the way of a good story. Samuel would die in 1801 and be buried northeast of Philadelphia.

At least two of my family lines were a part of the English effort to rule Ireland. The Jacksons came during a 300-year effort to use English farmers to subject the Irish. By 1725 nearly 25,000 had been relocated to Ireland from Scotland as an additional effort. This is the period identified by Allen with English importation of displaced from the Scottish Lowlands and other areas impacted by a famine. He cites sources that put the number of vagrants to be as high as 200,000 by 1700 nearly 1 in 10 of the population.

---

[6] Myers' work provides the information of this section of Jackson history.

Britain's efforts to rule Ireland had one major obstacle—the Irish who refused to be ruled. The British failed to co-opt Irish leaders to implement their policies. The cultures of the two-people clashed at several major junctions. The English society fostered a political system built upon ascending loyalties to leaders who provided protection for segments of the population. In Ireland a tribal society persisted. Allegiance to the clan surpassed any other.

We will consider two examples. The English could never overcome Irish differences in family and criminal justice. The families in England that were supported most by social order were those of noble families. These families existed to maintain social order by achievement. They amassed wealth and reputation. The first-born son held a position superior to other children. As heir, his inheritance was as much obligation as opportunity. He was tasked with the responsibility to build on family wealth and reputation. Other sons were insurance in case of the death of the first-born. Otherwise they fended for themselves generally interring the military or the church. Daughters contributed to family through their virtue. Virgin daughters were married to extend a networking that benefited the family.

Through the clan structure more Irish families were the objects of and participated in the social order. All sons benefited from the inheritance. This practice worked against building large fortunes, but dramatically enhanced social solidarity. The same can be said for the Irish practice of fostering. Families often foster children to build relationships across the clan. Frequently they were so absorbed into the family that it was difficult to distinguish between birth and foster children.

English families valued the purity of their line. Irish families valued the strength of the clan.

In England criminal justice was the keeping of the king's peace, always the measure of behavior against a list from outside. Sentencing was punishment for breaking the king's peace. Irish criminal justice was designed to maintain a communal peace. Crime broke the relationship between members of a clan or the relationship between clans. Punishment was an attempt to satisfy a grievance. Without satisfaction, the greater fear was revenge that could spiral into chaos.

Failing to rule through co-option, Allen asserts that the English moved to destroy the Irish social order.

> ...the colonizing power institutes a system of rule of a special character: designed to deny, disregard and delegitimate the hierarchical social—tribal, kinship—distinctions previously existing among the people brought under colonizing rule. The members of the subjugated group, stripped of their tribal and kinship identity, are rendered institutionally naked to their enemies, completely deprived of the shield of social identity and the corresponding self-protective forms of the tribal and kinship associations that were formally theirs. [The objective] is social death for the subjugated group as a whole.[7]

Since early in the 1600s England faced multiple Irish revolts in response to colonial policies and poor economic conditions that continually diminished prospects for the Irish. Their first attempt to alter the balance of power was the importation of English settlers. This failed primarily for two reasons: Irish land was less productive than English and an economic recovery in England made living conditions there more attractive to the settlers than what they were experiencing in Ireland. They started returning to England.

When John Morrison was among the Scots imported by the English to Ireland it was a second attempt to subjugate the Irish. Allen contends that through the importation of outsiders the English were attempting to create a "control stratum" to accomplish what their efforts at co-optation had failed to do: subjugate the tribal system. The Scots became a large mass of people brought in to accomplish the design of the elites to maintain subjugation of the Irish. The same process will be exported

---

[7] Allen, p. 35

to North America.

Allen lists four essential operating principles that the British learned in Ireland and later implemented in Jamestown.

1. **The oppressor group must be in the majority**. This might be called the Sir William Perry principle, after the person who first formulated it. This principle may incidentally serve to give racial oppression a "democratic" gloss.

2. From this "majority principle," and from the pyramidal structure of class society, it follows that **the majority of the oppressor group is necessarily composed not of members of the exploiting class, but an intermediate social control stratum of laboring classes, non-capitalist tenants, and wage-labors.**

3. **These laboring-class members of the oppressor group are to be shielded against competition of the members of the oppressed group by the establishment of economically artificial "anomalous" privileges**—artificial because they subordinate short-term private profits to considerations of social control.

4. Just as the system of capitalist production presents cyclical crises and regeneration, so **the system of racial privileges of the laboring classes of the oppressor group is adapted and preserved, come what may of the economic crisis, impoverishment, famine, intramural conflict, natural calamity or war, in order to maintain the function of the intermediate buffer social control stratum.**[8]

We should not be surprised that the English settlers in Jamestown bring their social habits to this new setting. Their social context was an English perspective of European society. They came of age in an era impacted by significant loss of life to the plague—from 1/5 to ½ of the population. In this era war was constant. The economy had dramatically shifted from traditional farming to cash focused farming and herding.

---

[8] Ibid, pp. 134-135 (emphasis added)

Impoverished peasants in England and Scotland were at various times forced into limited-term bond labor. Worse, in 1547 a law was passed enabling other English subjects with property to enslave indigent peasants. It was such a repugnant idea that by 1550 it was repealed.

The English elites believe that their freedoms had been restricted by the consequences of the plague. The dramatic loss of life resulted in a dramatic decrease in available labor. For more than 200 years the elites had struggled to keep wages in their favor. The peasants resisted. The peasant revolts are the more dramatic of those efforts. On a daily basis wages and social control represented the ongoing class of life-worlds.

Allen[9] references the emergence of a yeoman class during the reign of Henry VII (1485-1509) as a significant new factor in the social context. The yeoman emerged from the ranks of free-holding land families. They were enlisted to oversee the daily life of a new social order. The felt need for "supervisory and enforcement functions performed at the parish level" needed a new set of functionaries "constables, church wardens, Overseers of the Poor, jailers, directors of houses of correction, etc."

This new stratum of low-level administration soon provided an essential civic function. They provided more effective social control over the former peasants who were increasingly becoming homeless and wage less. In exchange for this service to the elites, the yeomen gained expanded opportunity: "they were entitled to vote for their shire's member of Parliament. Of far more importance was their right to apprentice their sons to lucrative trades and commerce, and to send their sons to schools and universities. But like the civic duties to which they were assigned, these privileges were theirs because, and only because, of their property status."[10]

The failure of the slave law indicated the failure of existing patterns of

---

[9] Allen (1997) vII, pp, 17-19
[10] Ibid, p19

social management during such a radical period of social change. The elites were pushing to assure their dominance in all things English. But workers needed wages. The peasant revolts were a clear indication that large numbers of subjects were less and less likely to acknowledge the legitimacy claims of the elites in their lives. The yeoman solution was important but not sufficient to manage the situation. The emerging capitalists interest needed a steady supply of labor, the cheaper the better.

In April 1563 a new legitimating structure was made law. The Statute of Artificers established the mandate for employers to pay workers agreed wages and for unemployed workers to accept any employment offered. This law would regulate English employment relations until 1813. To be certain, this law did not establish an equitable balance. The advantage did not rest with the workers.

> The oppressive intent of the Statute of Artificers was obvious on the face of it. In a situation made especially difficult by the oversupply of labor, workers were compelled to work for whatever the employing class, through the magistrates, chose to offer, and to forgo any improvement through individual or collective bargaining. By both its general and its apprenticeship provisions the statute consigned the generality of the wage-earning population to agricultural labor. Women workers were excluded from apprenticeship and made to serve in the lowest-paid drudgery. The severest censures of the anti-vagabond laws were threatened against the worker who sought to move from one place to another to improve his lot, unless bore the magistrate's certificate of permission. Yet oppressive as that law was, neither its contrivers nor its victims would believe that within several short generations, in a "New Albion," English workers would be worked as unpaid chattel bondmen and bondwomen, bought and sold from hand to hand for long terms of years, denied the

> right to marry, their children "bastards" by definition—
> and that such would be the common lot (not a real
> apprentice in a hundred) under "the custom of the
> country!"[11]

The English society that put these pieces in place for the elites in Jamestown had legitimated the shifting of land from small holders to those who would operate large cash-oriented farming schemes. The suppression of civil and political rights of the landless poor legitimated forced labor. These oppressions also restricted the ability of the landless to choose where they would live and the ability of parents to exercise authority over their children. This England legitimated different life-worlds for the elite and the others.

Jamestown was the first of a series of settlements England launched in the New World, primarily for economic and political purposes. Their first business plan called for obtaining gold, silver, and furs from the native population. It did not materialize. This plan clearly did not build on much knowledge of Virginia. Expectations were such that between 1607 and 1622 the vast majority of immigrants were from the genteel classes—working was not their intention. They expected to gain wealth rather than create it.

After 15 years, the Company business plan of exploiting native populations through trade or aggression was deemed a failure. The founders of Jamestown knew that their assignment required a structuring of the physical world they were entering. Their goal was straightforward: earn a profit for the investors and benefit the crown. Their first business plan failed because the environment of Virginia was not conducive to gold and silver mining and only minimally more so to furs.

Faced with abandoning the colony, the monoculture of tobacco became the primary focus of their second plan. Virginia land required transformation from wilderness to tillable conditions. Labor suitable to

---

[11] Ibid p. 24

implementing their plan in Virginia became a constant concern. All the available land was occupied by various tribes of the Powhatans.

English relations with the local Powhatan Society reproduced the mistakes of the Irish experiment. English efforts to trade for goods failed. The Powhatans were not sufficiently interested in the goods being offered to them. Their economy was "3/4 hunting, fishing and gathering; ¼ cultivation with no livestock."[12] In actuality the Powhatans had little visible wealth that appealed to the English, except labor. Some natives would sell those captured in raids as slaves to the English. The costs of converting native labor to an effective work force was too great. Natives resisted the working conditions, the work itself, and the English could find no reasonable solution for converting them into reliable labor. The English restricted the freedom of the natives and North America proved to expansive for containing native populations long enough for change to be profitable. Captives produced poor work outcomes. Also, they ran away. Once away from the settlements they blended in with the native population and were hard to recover. Finally, whatever the causes, the native population began to decline in the area and that decline increased with each year after 1607. As in Ireland the tribal system of local labor frustrated the English.

This failure only slightly altered the plan. The critical issues were clear:

(1) How to secure an adequate supply of labor
(2) How to establish and maintain the degree of social control necessary to assure the rapid and continuous expansion of their capital by the exploitation of that labor.[13]

They turned to England for the labor they needed. Bond service was used to entice some, like my ancestor William Logsdon, to envision a new life in Virginia. My 6x great grandfather through my father's paternal grandmother was William Logsdon. He was born in

---

[12] Ibid, p. 35
[13] Allen (2) p. 3

Bedfordshire, England in 1663. He agreed to a 4-year term of indenture as an eleven-year-old, arriving in Maryland in 1674. Foul winds diverted his ship from its Virginia destination. He worked off his indenture and bought 300 acres on the Maryland-Pennsylvania border. He raised tobacco as a cash crop to supplement his other farming ventures. In 1702 he purchased a wife. Honora O'Flynn was a captive from Ireland who was aboard a ship of women destined as wives for settlers. She agreed to the arrangement with the caveat that a priest be found first.

For a few like William it worked. They served their years, obtained land, and created a life for themselves. Bond service was also a means of transferring criminals from England to somewhere else. The vast majority of bond-laborers were prisoners who were sold to the Company or individuals kidnapped off the streets of English cities and sold to ship captains who resold them in Virginia. You can see that these servants would come with more challenges. It is the last group that had the most right to resent the bond servant system. Honora O'Flynn represented a significant group who entered bond servanthood through abduction.

> The "servant-trade" as it came to be called, that is, the export of chattel laborers from Europe, sprang us as a response to the profit-making needs of the tobacco business and it soon became a special branch of commerce; these bond-laborers "provided a convenient cargo" for ships going to the plantations to fetch tobacco, sugar, and the other raw products available.[14]

The Company men, the elite, took numerous other steps to maximize their return on investment. Small holders and tenets were forced into the wage labor pool through the limitations placed on tobacco production. Chattel servants were frequently found guilty of violating their contracts with an extension of time on their term as punishment. The company men took steps to limit their competition and maximize

---

[14] Ibid. p. 119

their opportunities for faster returns on investment.

The need to maximize return on investment became the controlling goal for the decisions reached by these actors in the formative years of Virginian society and by extension colonel life. The social system they created while seeking to maximize return created more advantage for company men (until the company's demise in 1624) than any other classification of immigrant. As could be expected the early advantage place the former company men at the center of colonial Virginia's politics and economy.

In or about 1628 references began to appear in the historical record referring to laborers as chattel.[15] Chattel is property. Property that can be purchased, sold, bartered, even used to pay off debts. Bond-laborers became chattel at the point their contracts were transferable. This system is in place by the arrival of the first African laborers in August of 1619.

George Yeardley traded for 20 or so Africans from a Dutch ship. His acquisition included women as well as men. They came into a system of transferable bondage that was a time-limited term of service. This system was applied to Yeardley's and subsequent African laborers for a considerable period. It was with English laborers that the first step towards a system without limits that passes from mother to child occurred.

The chattel system cost English bond-laborers considerable standing as English subjects. The Virginia Company knowingly reduced the civil liberties of fellow English subjects because of their more compelling goal: maximizing the return on investment.

Between 1607 and 1682, 92,000 Europeans migrated to Virginia. Allen identifies three-fourths of these as chattel-bond laborers. Each of these came with a limited-term contract that usually granted them land and other benefits at the fulfillment of the contract. Minimum terms of

---

[15] Ibid. p. 58

service were seven years but could be as much as 15 years. The contract was a civil arrangement. The breach of the contract was a criminal offense. Virginia courts readily extended the term of service for even minor offenses.

Africans arrived without a such a contract. They shared use of the English laborer's limited-term contract which shaped the experience of Africans for almost 60 years. The presence of free Africans in Virginia, Maryland, and later North Carolina, Georgia, and other colonies is possible because of the use of the limited term contracts. Not accounting for personal prejudice, the systematic differentiation between Africans and Christians (as the English referred to themselves) was not to appear until late in the century. During this period little seems to distinguish between bond-laborers who have completed their term.

The tactic of using social control strategies to reduce labor costs appears in the regulations structuring sexual interaction and marriage. The religious attitudes against mixed marriage was evidently not a strong deterrent. Neither were the 1640 laws which punished all bond-laborers who desired to marry by extending the length of their servitude. These statutes did not prohibit mixed African and English marriages.

Historical evidence does not demonstrate a popular outcry against these marriages. In 1662 a law was initiated by the elites to make mixed marriages a crime. The statutes stated its intentions to ban sexual relations between 'Christians and negros.' The search for lower wage costs had brought the elite to the point of attempting to control the bodies of their laborers.

Within this 1662 statute was a clause that demonstrated the elites' push for greater control: matrilineal servitude. The result of this clause, the children of bond-laborers become chattel bond-laborers at birth. The expectation is that they will remain in the service of the landowner until their twenties. With this clause women and their children lose civil liberties and increase in value: to the value of the direct labor women provide is added the potential labor of their offspring.

English tradition and English law regarded the status of children through their father. The 1662 Virginia statute should be regarded as social innovation motivated by the pursuit of profit, but with significant corollary impact. The loss of civil liberties impacts English women. The greater impact will be on the African women and their children, even though it will take more than twenty years. The 1662 legislation is a major step along the road to the creation of race in North America.[16]

The construction of differences, the assigning of relative value of persons, and the abridgement of English civil rights are social actions taken in pursuit of a common social end: maximizing profits or return on investment by controlling labor costs within their system of production. With legislation beginning in the 1690s this process has generated another social fact: differentiating between white and negro.

Prior to 1691 the elite referred to themselves and fellow Europeans as Christians. They referred to Africans as negros. In the 1691 statute sexual concourse between white women and negro men resulted in both being punished; between white men and negro women only the woman was punished. Other negative changes directed at negros related to residence. Any mixed couple had just three months to leave the colony. Any landowner that freed additional African bond-laborers had to make arrangements for them to depart the colony within three months.

The events that became known as Bacon's Rebellion (1676) originate in the system of small-holders created by the elite to meet two needs: a buffer community that protected against raids from the natives and which reduced the frequency of bond-laborers running away from their masters. Nathaniel Bacon, a recent immigrant who was in possession of considerable land holdings, took notice of the condition of the small-

---

[16] Martino, pp. 54-60

holders, caught between the Powhatans and the elite. He organized the small-holders and they began raiding the Powhatans in order to increase the land available to these small-holders on the western frontier.

The Powhatans fought back. The Colonial Council who had never been keen on the raids provided minimal assistance when the Powhatans made several key advances. Bacon then led his band to advance on the Council. This level of unresponsiveness led Bacon to demand a more representational council. In response the Colonial Council retreated across the Chesapeake to the eastern shore and to send for reinforcements from England. Bacon died before the Rebellion ended in failure.

Bacon's Rebellion revealed several social and political facts about the colony. Class distinctions existed between the elite in possession of plantation sized holdings who also controlled the political force of the Colonial Council and everyone else. The everyone else included freed bond laborers (English and African), other small holders, and current bond-laborers. The events of the Rebellion left no doubt that the elites did not possess the level of social control they desired. The coalition of the everybody else demonstrated the common cause that existed across this category. This common cause could unite and empower forces the elite needed to control. The Native Americans were outside the system and victimized by exclusion. I ask you to recall that Great Grandpa William had only served two of his years of indenture when Bacon's rebellion began.

Following Bacon's Rebellion, the decisions of Virginia's ruling elite reflect the influence of Virginia's history and the English context we discussed earlier. Following the social habits developed in the English experience in Ireland, in dealing with the landless peasants, and in managing the social disruption of a new economy, the Council identified these issues:

1. Controlling labor costs which threatened the success of their monocultural agriculture economy.
2. Securing a supply of labor that would fit cost constraints and meet the need for the expanded production.
3. Managing a working-class hostile to their social and economic objectives.
4. Justifying their worth to England.
5. Assuming physical survival in the face of challenges from the Native population, food supplies, and social conflict.

We have seen that context structures our world. Freedom is the capability to detect the characteristics of our social world and use that knowledge to initiate action to achieve objectives. Social control is the capability to influence how others define and take action in a given social world. Oppression is control that either reduces or removes the capability of others to take action. Social control is a legitimate operation within a society that promotes the well-being of its members. Oppression is not. It is the blatant disregard of the well-being of one or more groups within a society to increase the well-being of another group.

English society and its Virginia sub-set were not concerned with the well-being of all its members. This is critical in examining the social and economic development of Virginia between 1680 and 1750. The Virginia ruling elite faced difficult days with significant challenges to the colony and to their position within that colony. The economic challenges of land (quality and quantity) and controlling labor (supply and costs) were complicated by the social challenge of a population that recognized the legitimacy of the ruling elite to rule and create a social order to which they would give allegiance.

Habits are not made from legislation. The elite in Virginia may not have consciously set on this course, but they had to disrupt the reflexive monitoring habits of the small holders and indentured bond laborers. Bacon's Rebellion had revealed the common cause of these groups. This pattern of recognized shared interests had to be altered to assure social stability or at least this appears to be the motivation of the elites. The legislation during this period establishes a legitimate division of the interests of the African workers from the English.

In 1680, four years after the Rebellion, the tobacco market recovered from its latest down-turn. The militia formed after the Rebellion had removed the threat from the Powhatan which freed tensions on the margins of the colony. The opportunity for expanded planting and for greater market demand generated a fresh demand for cheap labor.

The Council had learned its lesson. It took steps to weaken the common cause between English and Africans, particularly bond-laborers. In 1682, the elites took two major steps. First, the legalization of life-time bondage, slavery, for African bond-laborers was legislated. Second, the Council began importing additional Africans to meet the demand for labor during the economic expansion.

Additionally, the Council began an information program to increase the fear level of colonialist and to increase the likelihood that the focus of that fear would center on the Africans. African participation in Bacon's Rebellion became the pretext for building a narrative that emphasized the violent nature of Africans. The manufactured fear was then used to legitimize the creation of "patrols" to protect colonialists from growing dangers. These patrols had a dual purpose. They policed the marginal areas and marginal groups. The patrols became a legitimate force used by the Council to divide and conquer the "everyone else" who had demonstrated that the real threat was that posed by the Council.

The Council began a process in which white and black came to inhabit different social worlds while occupying the same physical space. Critical to this process was de-linking of white knowledge of Africans from their knowledge of the social space occupied by Africans. The Council's efforts began a process of transferring fears experienced by the small-holders to a generalizing fear based on a projection of what people in bondage could do to secure freedom. Couple this with the social marginalization of Africans by means of legal and social control that reduced the status of any African below that of any white colonialist and subject to the whim of any white.

Martinot sees the participation of the lower-class whites in patrols as an issue of allegiance

> The concept of race emerged from this reconfiguration of allegiance and a concomitant shift from identification as English to identification as white. Out of a confluence of slavery, the purity concept, matrilocarity, paranoia, and organized political terror, the English settlers produced for themselves a sense of white nationality.

And so Whiteness began. In the next chapter I will discuss whiteness within a larger perspective of white privilege and white supremacy, for now our focus directs attention to the emergence of the construct and the consequences.

The Council has exercised its power to divest English subjects of their social and civil rights. It is not surprising that they will create a new condition in which slavery can take root and flourish if they are convinced it is in their self-interests. The post Rebellion period is not 1447 England. Africans are not English subjects. Besides the social habits of ruling elites allowed for self-interests to trump public well-being.

> The effect of setting aside the African population as a juridically ostracized category was to construct a social consciousness on the part of all English of a commonality against the Africans...[17]

The elements which resulted in the 'setting aside the African population' in American society are not sufficient individually to achieve the racial structuring that occurred. Each element is necessary, but alone they are solitary social events. They are bricks scattered about unless shaped into a wall. Just as bricks need mortar to fashion them

---

[17] Martinot, p. 64

into a wall, the elements created by the Council needed whiteness to form them into a demarcation between English and African bond-laborers.

The yeoman class innovation coupled with the Irish plantation experiences served the Council as social resources to resolve their social control problem—the over-identification of white bond-laborers with Africans. They created social distance between these groups by establishing preferential treatment for poor whites and initiating debilitation constraints on Africans.

The life-world of Africans brought to Virginia did not resemble the one created by the English. When the Council began importing Africans directly from Africa those differences became the basis for increasing social distance. All cultural habits: language, tribal customs, patterns of social status, family, marriage, and self-determination were destroyed in Virginia. The ethnocentrism of the English expressed itself in the description and meaning assigned the traits ascribed to the Africans. Some of the traits: low intelligence, childishness, uncivilized, and ignorance were harsh enough and ill-informed. Other traits ascribed: bestial and non-human reveal the lengths to which English/European elites would go in order to promote their self-interests.

The reality of differing life-worlds for white elites and poor whites required the total separation between those considered white and those not if the social and economic goals of the Council were to be achieved. To maintain this separation the elites needed this social adaptation, whiteness. The 'yeoman adaptation' is most clearly seen in the 1727 organization of 'slave patrols' to police the social divide.

> The job of the patrols was to maintain bond-laborer discipline around the plantations and enforce the slave codes. This meant watching for and capturing runaways, suppressing any appearance of personal autonomy in a slave, and watching over or suppressing group activity by slaves....Through the patrols, poorer

> whites acted as shock troops and commandos under elite leadership to guard and protect white society against the elite-proclaimed threat of "Negro Rebellion."[18]

The social system change desired by the elites was the shift in the poor whites associating with Africans as fellows with a common cause to associating with the elites as fellows defending against a common enemy. This takes places despite the fact that the poor whites continue to inhabit a very different economic life-world than that of the elites.

> Though the poorer whites remained economically marginal and politically disfranchised, their enrollment in the patrols provided an avenue of participation, a limited citizen franchise with respect to governance, a role of policing rather than making policy. As an institutionalization of the power of paranoia, the patrols kept powerless whites constrained to the colony and hard at work by giving them that role, if not rule. Elite control was exercised through granting power to control, and planter hegemony took the form of white solidarity.

This chapter is too long to detail all the historical markers for the development of this social system in colonial America. The clearest marker that these changes become American social habits can be seen in the compromises made during the Constitution Convention and codified in the Constitution. The promises of the Declaration of Independence do not apply to slaves. Come to think of it when written and adopted they do not apply women or even to white males who do not own property. How did such a social arrangement not result in open revolt by poor whites. The habit was so ingrained to become, in Giddens' words, "an unacknowledged condition of action."

---

[18] Ibid. p. 67

3 CASTE: ENFORCING THE HABIT OF AVOIDANCE

By 1936 slavery had been abolished for more than 60 years. My parents were just starting school. Four field researchers were concluding one and a half years of anthropological research sponsored by Harvard University and later publish as *Deep South: A Social Anthropological Study of Caste and Class*.[19] Two couples,

> A white fieldworker and his wife, and a Negro fieldworker and his wife lived in the society for a little over one and one-half years. All of the field workers except the white woman had been born and reared in the South or in the border states, living there continuously except during their college or university training....they conformed to the behavioral modes of their respective castes; ...The methodological aim from the beginning was to see every Negro-white relationship from both sides of the society, so as to avoid a limited "white view" or a limited "Negro view."[20]

This book is written with the University of Chicago style and detail of

---

[19] Davis, A., B.B. Gardner and M.R. Gardner. (1939). *Deep South: A Social Anthropological Study of Caste and Class*. Chicago: University of Chicago Press
[20] Ibid p. viii

Whyte's *Street Corner Society*. The working premise of the methodology behind these works is the need to develop 'thick descriptions' through intensive and long-term observation. Their observations indicated a society with clear demarcation between white and black residents to such an extent that "any physical relations of Negros and whites in Old City are controlled not by their genetic structure but by social traditions organized into a social system which allows and forbids certain actions."[21] Their conclusion, the American social system of the South and some of the north fit the designation of a caste system. Their conclusions were not well received within the social science community.

Sociology and anthropology in the 1930s were emerging social sciences primarily developing in Europe and the United States. A major concern for both disciplines was and is the stratification patterns in societies and what those patterns imply for the members of the society. Class is seen as the stratification pattern of societies developing a capitalistic (and through implication—modern) economic system. Class is a fluid category in which people of like wealth, income and tastes coalesce into social groupings which will act out of similar interests. Caste is a stratification pattern associated with traditional societies, most commonly India. Caste is a designation one acquires at birth and which is reinforced throughout the social order.

Some years later Berreman compares the social relations between 'touchables' and 'untouchables' in India with that between 'Negros' and 'whites' in southern America. He determines that both are caste systems with

> a hierarch of endogamous divisions in which membership is hereditary and permanent. Here the hierarch includes inequality both in status and in access to goods and services. Interdependence of the subdivisions, restricted contacts among them, occupational specialization, and/or a degree of cultural

---

[21] Ibid p. 8

distinctiveness might be added as a criteria, although they appear to be correlates rather than defining characteristics.[22]

As the years passed the caste approach was surpassed by a more traditional class approach to social stratification in the United States. The reasons for this shift are debatable, the consequences are not. If we understand our society as totally a class system, then the approach we take to inequality will be different than if we understood that we were addressing inequalities structured by caste.

The American situation is confusing. Utilizing the dual perspectives of their study, Davis concluded that the society of the south was parallel class systems inside a caste structure. In other words, American society consists of a white caste and a black caste. Within those caste distinctions operates separate class structures for each. Seeing the impact of class on all, we can avoid the actual situation that for most of our history those class structures were operating under different rules and with limited outcomes for those in the black caste.

The Virginia Colonial Council did not set out to create a caste system of stratification, but that is what they did. The measures they initiated to establish social control after Bacon's Rebellion created a pattern of white-black interaction and separation that established caste distinctions between the two categories. Their desire to separate the common cause of African bond-laborers and white bond-laborers succeeded beyond their expectations. Their actions were foundational to the social structure that we recreate each and every day.

Berreman, whose research spanned more than a year in Sirkanda, northern Uttar Pradesh, India, characterizes caste as a system with 'rigid rules of avoidance.' Davis documents this avoidance

...to the whites, the subordination of the Negro is not

---

[22] Berreman, G.D. "Caste in India and the United States" The American Journal of Sociology, Vol. 66, No. 2 (Sep., 1960). P. 121-122

merely a characteristic of the social structure, which might conceivably be subject to change, but is based upon immutable factors, inevitable and everlasting. To them, the Negro is a lower form of organism, biologically more primitive, mentally inferior and incapable of learning, and animal-like in his behavior.[23]

With short historical memories white Americans forget the designations our caste made for the black caste. The purpose of these designations was to imbed fear and antipathy for the black caste. These are socially created fears and antipathies. To sustain a social structure the propaganda of the Virginia Colonial Council had to become beliefs, support by religion and education. The beliefs were reinforced through personal behavior and public policy. The designation of caste was reinforced through sanctions for any, white or black, who challenged the 'rigid rules of avoidance.'

The avoidance is evident during all phases of US history, but nowhere more than in the Jim Crow patterns of 'separate but equal' water fountains, seating on trains and buses, restaurant and hotel facilities, housing, schools, and worship.

The avoidance is possible in both India and in the US because

> …high castes maintain their superior position by exercising powerful sanctions, and they rationalize their status with elaborate philosophical, religious, psychological, or genetic explanations. The latter are not sufficient in themselves to maintain the systems, largely because they are incompletely accepted among those whose depressed position they are thought to justify. In both places castes are economically interdependent. In both there are great differences in power and privilege among, as well as class differences

---

[23] Davis, p. 15-16

within, castes and elaborate barriers to free social intercourse among them.[24]

Davis reinforces and expands on this observation.

> All the social structures in the society operate to reinforce the caste system—associations, churches, the courts, even the schools and the Negro class system—for none of these challenges the fundamental separate, endogamous nature of the two caste groups. Relations between Negroes and whites generally proceed smoothly, with each group playing its "proper" role. Habit and the law are not the only sanctions for conformity, however; upon occasion, direct physical punishment is used "to keep the Negroes in their place."[25]

Resistance to their proper role had characterized Africans from the time of their arrival. Slavery in the Colonies stripped Africans of everything but physical life. As Africa faded on the eastern horizon, so did the culture, family, and home of the captives. When slave holders implemented a pattern of separating slaves from the same tribe, the isolation of the captive became complete. Resistance to the conditions of slavery was anticipated by slave owners. The degree of violence used on plantations to keeps slaves compliant was not consistent or universal across all plantations. Runaways were subject to death at the hands of the patrols. Slaves who were perceived to exceed the status of their caste assignment were subject to violence. Any black male accused of inappropriateness to white women likely suffered severely. After the Civil War the patrols morphed into the Ku Klux Klan, lynch mobs did not morph, they had been around since the 1780s. Various sources report that more than 3,400 blacks have been lynched since 1882. Numbers before that are not known. The use of the term 'lynch' seems to have

---

[24] Berreman, p. 123
[25] Davis, p. 44-45

disappeared while killings have not. Violence has been a legitimate tool in the enforcement of America's caste system.

The avoidance or separation between the two castes is repeatedly affirmed and expanded by the courts, particularly the Supreme Court. In 1857 the court ruled on *Dred Scott v. Sanford*. Scott was seeking his freedom based on having resided in Wisconsin a non-slave state as defined by the Missouri Compromise. Chief Justice Taney wrote the decision. Scott was denied on the grounds that he nor any other descendent of Africans brought for the purpose of slavery could attain the status of citizenship. Scott was classified as property. Taney's opinion stated "a perpetual and impassable barrier was intended to be erected between the white race and the one which they had reduced to slavery, and governed as subjects with absolute and despotic power." African Americans were and always would be subjects of the white race and not citizens of the United States.

Because the Supreme Court overturned the Civil Rights Act of 1875 in 1883 and established that individual states held the power to establish civil rights, the way was cleared for another decision. In 1896 the *Plessy v. Ferguson* decision, a Louisiana law that established 'separate but equal' as a basis for managing African Americans in public was determined to be Constitutional. The Supreme Court reinforced the pattern that States could not be limited by Constitutional guarantees to civil rights, well at least black caste civil rights. The need to maintain social distance found a new vehicle. The clear message to all, the states have the power to institutionalize segregation. The habits of avoidance were legitimated.

Legitimizing avoidance was not limited to the 19th century. Education challenges the boundaries of caste. Any number of examples can be presented. Note the avoidance in education in the 1973 decision, *San Antonio v. Rodriguez*, upholding school funding on the basis of local property taxes. Low income segregated housing values when the basis for funding public education maintain the caste characteristics of avoidance. The next year, in *Milliken v. Bradley*, halted school busing as a strategy to counter structures and habits of avoidance.

Some of you are asking yourselves why I have forgotten *Brown v. Board of Education* and other court rulings. I have not. I will deal with them in another context.

My research has led me to the conclusion that a two-caste system with class differentiation in both existed with the legitimation of state and federal government in colonies and the United States from 1682 until 1964. As destructive as this condition has been for all of us, the personal habits of avoidance, of separation, and of segregation have been far more destructive. The existence of this pattern of habits is evidence that the program of propaganda initiated by the Virginia Colonial Council to divide white from African bond-laborers succeeded beyond their expectations.

Davis devoted a considerable number of pages to the habits which controlled the sexual contact between whites and blacks. Their description reinforced the latent nature of caste. Only white men escaped extensive social backlash for exercising their choices. All others paid a heavy social cost. Sexual contact between white and black creates a child that could challenge the clear-cut lines between the castes. Except the American innovation of the one drop rule created a division between the castes, though not always enforceable, it was always demeaning.

The propaganda convinced whites that it was the will of God for blacks to be subject to whites. The blacks are inferior in all aspects: intelligence, industry, social skills, childlikeness or unable to assume responsibility. The caste system required very proscribed behavior by both whites and blacks. All of this to keep the proper social distance, to assure that both black and white stayed in their place.

I believe our failure to approach the 'racial' division in America with a realistic understanding of the caste nature of those relations has cost us dearly. I came of age in the modern Civil Rights Era. Our attitudes and the solutions that were legitimated in legislation approach the divisions as if blacks were only a social class. Legislation that mandated equal opportunity assumed blacks could change class like the rest of us.

Brown v. Board of Education (1954) mandated that 'separate but equal' could not provide equal education for blacks. The focus was on assuring equal educational opportunities. In 1958 the court reaffirmed this decision and weakened the position of local communities and states in *Cooper v. Aaron*. Desegregation of schools could not be avoided because of lack of local support by either officials or population even if it were expressed as violence towards the black students.

A major contributor to this misread, that blacks could be elevated in the class system of the US was my discipline of sociology. Noted sociologists, Park, Parsons, Simpson and Yinger disputed the thesis of Warner, Davis, and Berreman that US society was and is a two-caste / with classes system. Much of social theory assumed that the structures of 'racial' division would die under the weight of economic development and the expanding application of the American Creed (created equal— pursuit of life, liberty, and happiness).[26]

The Civil Rights Act of 1964 and the Voting Rights Act of 1965 were the legitimation framework established to dismantle the social distance which separated African Americans in public life. The Civil Rights Act addressed discrimination based on race, color, religion, sex, and national origin. Additionally, it was legislation providing structure to the *Brown v. Board of Education* decision. Public places were declared fully public. The Voting Rights Act restricted the methods states had put in place to limit the voting of African Americans. I will state again, legislation does not create habits. Rather, legislation frames a legitimation for behavior and creates avenues for redress if those behaviors are not met. In 1964, the Supreme Court upholds the Civil

---

[26] If you are interested the literature will provide more details. I suggest you start with Paul Metzger. "American Sociology and Black Assimilation: Conflicting Perspectives" in The American Journal of Sociology, Vol. 76, No. 4. (Jan., 1971), pp. 627-647.

Rights Act in two decisions *Heart of Atlanta Motel Inc. v. US* and *Katzenbach v. McClung.*

Because of expectations that sociology captured in the points I made above, we can see that the national leadership was unprepared and did not fully address the habits of segregation and discrimination (avoidance) that had developed over the almost 300 years since the Colonial Council had launched its assault on Africans to secure control over their society. These habits are so deeply seated in white Americans that we need Giddens' structuration theory to understand their unconscious nature in motivating ongoing discrimination. Three hundred years of habits do not disappear because of legislation.

In a 1971 decision (*Griggs v. Duke Power Co.*) the Supreme Court extended the reach of the Civil Rights Act to specifically include employer action that indirectly effected the employment of minorities and women. Human Resource policies could not eliminate these populations through unnecessary procedures designed to eliminate them from consideration for employment.

A final court decision we need to note is *Loving v. Virginia.* In 1967 the court finally delegitimized the regulation of interracial marriage. In fact, this ruling removed the criminal state these marriages placed the partners. Three hundred years we tolerated a society operated by ruling elites that we sanctioned through elections that considered it an illegal act to marry outside of one's caste.

African Americans recognized the hollow promise of the public decisions. They have lived every day with the subtle applications of caste that remain in effect to keep them in their place, their caste. White backlash resisted the dismantling of their privilege. Attacks on quotas, resistance to reverse discrimination and countless other adaptations were made to keep caste structures in place. Each is a means of re-directing the conversation from the ongoing issue of avoidance in our national caste structure.

Slowly, too slowly, whites are coming to grip with the reality that the *Deep South* research team uncovered more than 80 years ago.

> The caste system, as has been shown, controls and defines the relations between the two color groups and is the principal factor in the interactions between any Negro and any white. It is expressed not only in behavior but also in the concepts and ideologies of the groups. Furthermore, the caste system limits the variation from the caste dogmas and enforces the systems of control by which extreme variations are prevented or punished. It thus provides a very definite code of behavior by which every individual knows how he should act and what he can expect in his relations with the other group.[27]

African Americans have tired of a caste system that limited their membership in American society. The dominance of the white caste has assured that we did not have to live with the day-to-day realities of caste. The presence of a class structure within each caste has allowed whites to ignore the actual problem, we perpetuate our position of dominance with subtle acts of avoidance maintaining the age-old objective: keeping the black caste in their place.

White America overestimates the progress we assume from the 1960's legislation. We have removed many of the overt, offensive behavior in our cross-caste contact. We have passed legislation to address class issues without tearing down the walls of avoidance that perpetuates caste. My family were willing participants in the white caste of America. That history can only be owned. If we are to alter our history, then our task is to bring whiteness out of the unconscious sections of our being and recognize how it motivates our actions. The following chapter takes up issues of whiteness.

---

[27] Davis, p.57

4 FREE, WHITE, AND TWENTY-ONE

> ...white workers deployed black workers (through exclusion) [to certain jobs and job categories] to create whiteness for themselves as a social value, a social property, a form of social capital. Whiteness became a form of property right, valorizing all associated with it in relation to blacks, who were in all senses left propertyless...the concept of race marks a social structure rather than a biological characteristic. It is in fact a property relation, a mark of social status that differentiates those with (the) property from those without it.[28]

As a child, well, all our shared lives actually, I was mesmerized by the storytelling of my mom's dad, Monroe Morrison. His stories were all about family. He told stories about people I knew and about family that neither of us knew except by the stories. Most of the stories centered on the Morrisons, Manes, and Watts, the family lines he knew from their time in Arkansas. The stories related struggle. He didn't hide the blemishes, even the evil. He made sure that I knew the people I came from.

Grandpa did not have stories from most of my ancestors though. The

---

[28] Martinot p. 97

following are the lineages that have bundled together to produce my sisters and me. For most there are no grandpa stories. The details of their lives are reduced to census data, military records, and a few personal details. They have contributed to our physical and social selves. I introduce them by surname as they entered our family bundle.

Jackson / Morrison

Hall / Watts

Goodman / Hicks / Manes / Goodnight

Kittle / Reece / Martin / Moody

Bradley / Cornett / Wood / Sampley / Begley

Chaffin / Howard / Mosby / Smart / Lawson / Smith / Dowdy

Lightfoot / Davis / Fields / Darby

O'Flynn / Logsdon

James

Mee

Meadows

These 33 lines are the only ones identified in our research as being part of our American history. There are several unknown spouses whose lines we cannot identify. Their social habits influenced the socialization of the next generation. Every person in my bundle of lineages (me included) has responsibility for the actions they have taken. All lines were residents of slave states when they entered my biography. The Watts, Morrison, Manes, Goodnight, Martin, and Moody were residents of Arkansas before 1860. The Jacksons left Georgia spent a short time in Alabama and arrived in Missouri in 1872. As far as we know they all were farmers with some also serving public roles as pastors, justices of the peace, road supervisors, and law enforcement. Some of the farmers were reasonably successful, others were share croppers. Between 1674 and 1872 they were on the move. Almost every generation made at least one change in residence. For the most part their movements reflect the progression of the American frontier. Despite family lore, only the Watts have been identified as Native American. They were Cherokees and came to Arkansas in the 1830s as part of the Trail of Tears migration.

I assume that those who populated my family lines were people of their times. Hauerwass reminds us that, "All ethical reflection occurs relative to a particular time and place."[29] I offer this story realizing that my judgements are based on an ethic formed in the last 55 years. You should also know I assume that had I lived at any other time period my attitudes and behavior would be very different than those of today. If another storyteller emerges from my great or great-great grandchildren they will probably ask, "What was wrong with that Dwight Jackson? He claimed to see so much, but he was blind to something as simple as…."

My family has lived in the shadow of Jamestown. The consequences of the Council's decisions, both those that could be anticipated and those that could not became the building blocks of our history. History is the economic, social, psychological, and spiritual actions taken by members of a society as they create their lives, individual and corporate. Decisions taken to support the business plan of an English corporation had short-term gains for them and has cost my family and yours.

An unintended consequence of the Council was the creation of whiteness as a social category. When it first appeared in the records of the Virginia Colonial Council it was very precise: not black or Indian. Lately, the term whiteness is used with greater imprecision. If this was merely an academic conversation, it would not be a big deal. Participants would lay out their definitions and proceed to make their arguments. But, this isn't an academic discussion, it is the lives of my

---

[29] Hauerwass, S. (1983) The Peaceable Kingdom. Notre Dame: University of Notre Dame Press, p. 1

family. If the story stopped with me then I would be less concerned. The family that follows me contains people of African, Korean, and European descent. Given the social history of our nation these grandchildren may or may not be residents of the same life-world with each of them facing similar life-challenges. The persistence of whiteness threatens some of my grandchildren. This is not an academic issue for me, it is a consideration of how whiteness contributes to an uneven future for these kids I love. The first clues I had on my family's investment in whiteness came from, well who else, Monroe.

Monroe had seen more than 70 birthdays by the time Congress passed the Civil Rights and Voting Rights acts. We never talked about them. In fact, it was only three times that the subject of race came up. He made it clear to me one day as we were walking in town that blacks and whites should not marry. Another time when the news covered some incident of race conflict he said, "We have never had those problems in Stone County." Mom commented almost as an aside, "That's because all blacks within a hundred miles knew it meant their life to be there after sundown." I have never seen an African-American in my 67 years of visiting Stone County, Arkansas. He also told me about his membership in the Ku Klux Klan during the 1920s and 1930s. He offered little details and I didn't know enough to ask. His purpose was to let me know that the Klan were decent ordinary men who took care of those who would bring crime and dishonor on the community, white or black.

Monroe was born in St. Joe, Arkansas in 1893. His great-grandfather, Thomas Calvin Morrison, had moved from Tennessee (with a short stop of several years in Illinois) to Timbo valley in what is now Stone County, Arkansas before 1842. Thomas' grandson, John Cornett Morrison found a prospective wife 30 miles west in the community of St. Joe. He and Nellie Manes were married in January 1892. Monroe was their first child born the next year. John and Nellie would leave St. Joe for the more remote region of south Stone County to raise their family and seek their fortune.

Both sides of Monroe's family were mountain people. Searcy and Stone counties are in the Boston Mountains of the southern Ozarks. The Morrisons and Manes came from Tennessee, Kentucky, and North Carolina. They were true Scots-Irish. They were independent and used to settling their own affairs. Family lore is littered with gun fights and feuds. Both the Morrisons and Manes were avid members of secret societies: the Peace Society, the Masons, and the Klan.

Morrisons, Manes, and Monroe's future in-laws, the Watts, were active in the Peace Society of Searcy County. This secret organization existed across several counties in north central Arkansas. Many in this part of Arkansas considered neither Northern nor Southern causes worthy of war. John Campbell of Searcy County was one of five delegates to the Succession Convention to vote against leaving the Union on the first ballot. When he later changed his vote, he declared that he did so to protect the County from retribution. Later events substantiated his fear. When young men were ignoring the call to arms, a Confederate detail came to the area to 'conscript' recruits. The first 12 were marched in chains to Little Rock, a trip of 112 miles over 12 days.

Despite limited formal conflict, the War was hard on the people of this area and my family in particular. Two of Mom's great great-grandfathers were murdered by Jayhawkers. Thomas Calvin was killed in 1864 at his home outside of Timbo by men who believed he had gold buried in his garden. John Watts, one of Mom's maternal great great-grandfathers was kill in 1865 at his home in Rumley, a few miles south of Leslie. It was a different band of Jayhawkers. These were raiding out of the Indian Territory. The reason he was targeted has been a matter of dispute. There is evidence the raid was to settle an old feud that dated back to 1798. John's grandfather, Chief John Watts had led a force of 1,000 against what is now the city of Knoxville, Tennessee. At the end of this conflict he signed a treaty that put a portion of the Cherokee nation at a disadvantage. Both murders have also been tied to fact that multiple members of each family were members of the Peace Society. No one theory can be substantiated.

The area where my family made their living was and in many still is a very remote and sparsely populated. The only era of significant economic growth was a boom time between 1890 and the 1920s. Besides subsistence agriculture, natural resources were minerals and timber. Mining was located in the St. Joe area with some coal and metals mined in the Arlberg community. The St. Louis and Northern Arkansas Railroad (later the Missouri and North Arkansas) extended their line from Eureka Springs through Harrison, St. Joe, Marshall, and Leslie. The Dinky Line was a spur line from Leslie to Arlberg. This facilitated the transportation of mining and timber products from the Arlberg area.

The Manes worked in the mines of St. Joe. Monroe's stories in which they figured placed them in St. Joe and Marshall. Monroe's dad, John Cornett moved the family to the Meadow Creek area by 1907. This put the family business just north of Arlberg allowing them to take advantage of the Dinky Line for shipping timber. Great-grandpa was known as 'Black John the Sawmill Man.' Family history reports that at his peak he had seven sawmills employing over 1,100 men. He took Monroe out of school in the 3rd grade to apprentice him to a blacksmith at one of his mills. Black John's mills produced staves for barrels and cross ties for railroad construction. He cut the virgin white oak timber on the hills around Arlberg. White oak was used for both barrel staves and cross ties.

The boom brought industry to the county. The H.D. Williams Cooperage to Leslie from Popular Bluff, MO. It reached a production of 3,000 barrels per day. Mays Manufacturing produced staves for barrels. These fifteen or so years are an anomaly for Searcy County. Never again has the economy of the region been so robust. The beginning of the end of the boom was the passage of the 18th Amendment and the implementation of prohibition. Sure, the local moonshiners had an expanded market, but no whisky meant there was no need for whisky barrels. With the closing of Williams and Mays the county began to depopulate fast. In the next 100 years it would never regain this level of population nor level of income.

White Supremacy

The boom had another impact. For 40 years the small population of former slaves and their children, located primarily in Harrison, had been fairly stable. They were poor, and they knew to maintain proper deference to the white population. The shortage of labor gave them opportunity to get unheard of construction jobs on the railroad. Conflict followed.

The two outcomes were the planting of the Ku Klux Klan in Searcy County and two rounds of race riots, 1905 and 1909.

The population of the black community of Harrison was 115 at this time. The negotiated relationship was permanently altered by the railroad. Conflict over jobs was heightened as outsiders come to the area looking for work and discovering the competition the locals, black and white provided. Then the first rendition of the railroad, the St. Louis and Northern Arkansas went into receivership. The sudden unemployment seems to be one stress too many. In October of 1905 white mobs surged through the black community burning houses, shooting out windows, and ordering all blacks to clear out. Most did. Two days later a black railroad worker was shot and killed with no attempt to bring the killer to justice. In 1909 the violence was sparked when a black man was convicted of raping a white woman and sentenced to death. This time the violence in the black community drove out all but one old woman. Interestingly all sources of information from these times do not have detailed accounts—either governmental or press.

Given what I know of my family, given the way these issues were discussed, I cannot imagine that these events happened in their backyard and they were not in the middle of it. If I am right then my family, in this instance and possibly others, participated in acts of white supremacy. This is difficult to face let alone say, but it is part of a conversation that must take place. My family contributed to the enforced program of caste in America. It is very reasonable to expect that we contributed to the

> More than 4400 African American men, women, and children were hanged, burned alive, shot, drowned, and beaten to death by white mobs between 1877 and 1950. Millions more fled the South as refugees from racial terrorism, profoundly impacting the entire nation.[30]

The historical accounts I have consulted develop a compelling case that the Virginia Colonial Council believed that they had faced a situation of class conflict during Bacon's Rebellion. Their actions demonstrate that they were willing to do anything to avert another such crisis. They were willing to subvert the civil rights of English subjects. They were willing to do much more to Africans. It may be an inappropriate use of the term, but it feels like an act of violence to assassinate the nature of an entire segment of the population for their purposes. Mom tried to drill it into me that the end does not justify the means. Profit, fiscal survival, any of these ends did not justify this course of action.

I am not sure if we can measure the depth to which their program of paranoia has permeated the white caste. The fear that exists does so at the unconscious level of our motivations for action. Note the number of whites who confess to reacting in fear when they encounter a black man in a sketchy situation. This propaganda has been so successful that blacks confess to similar feelings.

What is the level of generalized fear that must exist for anyone to burn a child simply because of their skin color or that they demonstrated 'uppitiness?' In preparing I have read accounts of racial violence in Arkansas during the 1910s and 1920s that appears to have no other explanation than unabated paranoia. With no ability to account for the deaths of Africans in transport or of the violence experienced during slavery and stopping at 1950 the Lynching Museum can account for

---

[30] https://museumandmemorial.eji.org/

4,400 victims of white paranoia. I cannot account for my daughter's experience in the car chase from a basketball game except for unchecked paranoia. I cannot account for my bundle of family lines during this period. My sense of responsibility tells me that some of them were present during acts of violence that would shame me today.

If we are to eliminate the caste system in America, then we must engage in a conversation that is honest and promotes reconciliation and healing. I am writing this in July 2018. The last three years demonstrate that white paranoia remains a viable thread within our national fabric. It exists in sufficient measure that it can be a factor in national politics. People who believe in and practice racial violence need to be healed. Acts of intimidation and terror cannot be tolerated!

White Privilege

My family lines are populated by hard working folks. They were frontier people. Until the mid-20th Century they were farmers, miners, or loggers. More recently they have been skilled laborers and teachers. My generation has seen college graduates and a smattering of white collar workers. Most generations have had a preacher or two. Very little of what I know about my family would I associate with the term 'privilege.' We see privilege in those neighborhoods and circles of our communities where the lives of those folks seem much easier than ours. We were a Chevrolet family. We got by week to week, pay check to pay check and in tight times family stepped up to help. No, for us privilege was found in other neighborhoods where children attended private schools and had easy access to the best colleges, and jobs that paid you enough your family could go on vacation. Our folks left inheritances of stories and maybe a piece of land. Never did we have to worry about probate.

My family and I failed to see that those who saw white privilege grew up in families and neighborhoods where my life looked easy, fixed to a positive outcome. They failed to see the struggle our family had in the winter when there were no construction jobs, when the phone was turned off for lack of payment, and when mom and dad argued over the price of eggs. We failed to see that their life was like that most of the time. We both failed to see that the system had been rigged for a long time.

Pem Davidson Buck became an anthropologist because she was plagued by the structures of inequality that had shaped her life in Kentucky. *Worked to the Bone* is a historical/anthropological study of rural life in Kentucky. In her perspective white privilege is a series of social arrangements which convince middle and working-class whites to buy into an economic and political system that promises them advancement and advantage with minimum profit in order to secure allegiance to political and economic elites in a shared status of white. The first configuration of this promised advantage took the form of land.

We left my Quaker 6x great-grandfather Thomas buried in Pennsylvania. His son Nathan turns up in North Carolina. Nathan and his son Edward lived in close proximity to a Friend's Settlement. While family history would suggest a close relationship with this Friend's community no records exist to establish their religious community. Nathan is buried in the cemetery of the Sandy Creek Baptist Church just a bit further than the Friend's Meeting House from his home. Again, we have no record of any formal affiliation. Those descendent of Nathan whose religious affiliation all identify as Baptist. The church founded in 1755 still exists and is located a few miles west of Liberty, North Carolina. Sandy Creek and its founding pastor, Shubal Sterns are formational to Baptist life in the United States. Less Calvinistic they were aggressively evangelistic. Their program of church planting shaped the lives of those on the frontier of Virginia, North and South Carolina, and Georgia. Of possible more immediate interest for the Jackson saga is the relationship of the church to the Regulators.

The vast majority of the residents of Randolph County (home to Sandy Creek Baptist and Edward) and Guilford (home to Nathan) were yeoman farmers. The Crown governor, William Tyron was at best indifferent to the corruption of local administrators—sheriffs and tax collectors. Led by Quaker Herman Husband with full cooperation from the Baptist, local residents organized and attempted to get the governor to initiate reforms. He did not. The Regulators expanded to other counties and the problems persisted. Not all protests were within the law and the governor sent troops to deal with the situation. The Regulators were defeated in 1771. Public hangings of the leaders, including at least one member of Sandy Creek, were followed by the governor setting his militia on the farms of the Sandy Creek members, burning buildings and destroying crops and animals.

Nothing we have found indicates the involvement of Nathan or Edward. What we do know is that following the raids, those associated with Sandy Creek began to move westward. Edward appears to be among those making this move of about 100 miles showing up in Burke County (west of Hickory) sometime between 1782 and 1790. And he got land grants in 1802 and 1804. Edward's son Joseph received five land grants in western North Carolina. In 1825 Joseph moved his family (evidently other Jackson cousins made the move during the same period) to north Georgia. In 1827 and 1832 multiple Jacksons received land grants.

The Jackson clan was on the move. They were no different than other yeomen farmer families. The land to which they had access was frequently mountainous and of inferior quality. It was liberated Indian land. Buck details the process in Kentucky.[31] Wealthy land speculators ignored treaties to protect Indian land and secured ownership of the best land prior to its availability to others. Grants went to veterans of the Revolutionary War. Officer grants measured in the thousands of acres. Private soldiers' grants ranged between 100-300 acres. Black veterans were excluded from the process. With the army representing the class structure of the Eastern Establishment, the grants of land in

---

[31] Buck, p. 30

Kentucky never challenged the existing class power arrangements. We Jacksons received grants of land, but it doesn't feel like we were privileged. It is hard to argue that we didn't have certain advantages, though.

The slaves were at the bottom of this social arrangement. They resisted their treatment and oppression. Periodically throughout the period of slavery whites were killed by slaves. The propaganda launched by the Virginia Council after Bacon's Rebellion became fact. Buck cites research that puts slave revolts at 200.[32]

White advantage didn't feel that way in places where wages rather than land were the inducement used for their allegiance. From the 1830s to the Civil War labor and urban unrest marked the clear class struggle between workers and owners. The life of non-slave tenant farmers was equally miserable.

Buck suggests that the elites countered this growing dissatisfaction and unrest by altering the social arrangement.

> The initial construction of whiteness had been based on material benefits for Whites: land, or the apparently realistic hope of land. By the 1830s and 1840s, most families identified by their European descent had had several generations of believing their whiteness was real. But its material benefit had faded. Many Whites were poor, selling their labor either as farm renters or as industrial workers, and they feared wage slavery, no longer certain they were much freer than slaves.[33]

This was becoming serious. There were multiple signs that the social arrangement was fraying. The power elites, both economic and political, were unwilling to alter the material distribution system to lessen the

---

[32] Ibid, p. 53

[33] Ibid, p. 57

impact of poverty. A new propaganda program immerged that intended to alter the perception of race once again.

> The work of particular white intellectuals, who underscored the already existing belief in white superiority and the worries about white slavery, was funded by elites and published in the elite-owned printing houses. These intellectuals provided fodder for newspaper discussions, speeches, scientific analysis, novels sermons, songs, and blackface minstrel shows in which white superiority was phrased as if whiteness in and of itself was naturally a benefit, despite its lack of material advantage. This sense of superiority allowed struggling northern Whites to look down their noses at free Blacks and at recent immigrants, particularly the Irish. This version of whiteness was supposed to make up for their otherwise difficult situation, providing them with a "psychological wage" instead of cash—a bit like being employee of the month and given a special parking place instead of a raise.[34]

The "psychological wage" was reinforced through new measures to maintain the two-caste system, Jim Crow, separate but equal, and segregation. As a white male, when I look at the overt acts of violence necessary to maintain this social arrangement I can understand how my sense of advantage looks more and more like privilege.

Periodically the White working class have demanded protection in the job market. It began with legislation limiting the use of slaves in certain occupations. Unions were segregated for much of the active period of labor organization. In the twentieth century the Jacksons and Morrisons have made the transition to wage labor. My parents' generation were primarily skilled laborers: carpenter, electrician, plumber. I had an uncle on each side that continued to work in logging, one in Arkansas the

---

[34] ibid

other in Oregon. Several of my children have been successful in corporate management. White advantage has worked out well for us.

Whiteness

The propaganda program creating the "psychological wage" worked. This wage has maintained the two-caste system as well as any other aspect of our multiple social arrangements. This wage lines up with what we now call whiteness. An application of Giddens' structuration theory would suggest that whiteness lines up with Powell's concept of implicit bias. I consider implicit bias as a similar concept to the one I was trying to communicate to my students when I told them about my structural racism.

> Because we have conscious control over—or, indeed, access to—only a small part of the processes going on in our brains, many of our thoughts and feelings, even during waking hours, occur without our express command or permission. Although most of us are completely unaware of their influence on our subconscious, these biases affected how we perceive, interpret, and understand one another...Because these attitudes—unrecognized on the conscious level—influence choices and decisions, individual and institutional discrimination can and does occur even in the absence of blatant prejudice, ill will, or animus.[35]

Earlier we documented Supreme Court rulings that established whiteness as a property characteristic held by some members of US society and withheld from others. I am convinced that the implicit nature of whiteness keeps it hidden from many of us who are white.

---

[35] Powell, pp. 21-22

Whiteness is normal. Being white we accept our place in the social order, accept its normalcy. We fail to see the presence of whiteness as a definitive marker of the two-caste system of social stratification. We also fail to see how it impacts the distribution of membership and other social goods between whites and non-whites.

Conclusion

White supremacy, white privilege, and whiteness do not fall into the neat categories I constructed or even those constructed by anyone. Terms allow us to examine concepts and characteristics. I have used this structure hoping that the default response by we whites to this discussion might be avoided. Being white is more than acts of violence.

> The process of racialization has changed and is changing. The number of old-style explicit racists is declining. Even though we talk about white and non-white attitudes, a range of attitudes and conditions is reflected in each racialized group. What may be more interesting is that most of us carry conflicting racial attitudes within ourselves.[36]

Remember that my grandchildren provide my controlling motivation for this book and for the process that I now own as a significant part of my future. I want to contribute to the possibility that all of my grandchildren will inhabit the same life-world. With King I want children to be measured by more than the color of their skin. I want it badly enough to suffer the pain of examining my implicit biases.

In preparing this chapter I recalled several conversations, arguments, actually that took place more than 50 years ago. When dad thought

---

[36] Ibid

mom pushing him too hard in a direction he did not want to go the argument would come. She frequently backed him into a logical corner. His parting comment, "I am free, white, and twenty-one. I guess I'll just do as I please. Dad was being paid the "psychological wage" as late as 1958.

5 MISSED MOMENTS

For more than 300 years a habit of racialized action has been present in our country. This habit had developed and persisted because those in power created structures that legitimized this habit. The prevalence of this habit developed because tens of millions of Americans have utilized this habit daily as they have pursued personal goals. Yet, there have been key moments in our history when we could have changed the habit. Many would contend that the habit no longer has official backing and that fewer utilize the habit actively. Why then does it persist?

Moment One

In the days following Bacon's Rebellion the habit of racialization was not widespread nor established. The ruling elite of Virginia Colony was also the economic elite. Their response to the event and the purpose of these rebels began a process which established the habit of racialization.

> What Virginia's laboring-class people, free and bond, were fighting for in Bacon's Rebellion was not the overthrow of capitalism as such, but an end to the version of that system imposed by the plantation elite,

based on chattel bond-servitude and engrossment of land.[37]

The Virginia experiment was fundamentally different from the experience in Plymouth Bay. Plymouth was an economy of small farmers and artisans while Virginia was a plantation colony with a planter class that numbered no more than 5% of the Europeans in 1730. By 1676 the direction and priorities of this group were well known. The lack of Council support for the Indian phase of the Rebellion only reinforced the laboring-class' frustration with life in Virginia. Past events had continuously led to a lowering of opportunities for working people, particularly in light of the success of the elite in the 1620s to demote tenant farmers to the level of day laborers.

Allen clearly details the choices of the planter elite for a divide and conquer strategy with the laboring-class. He quotes Nash, "'In the late seventeenth century...southern colonizers were able to forge a consensus among upper- and lower- class whites...Race became the primary badge of status.[38] From the elite perspective the consensus was necessary to divide the numerically superior laboring-class through the separation of African from white. They had learned that the time needed to get military support from England was so long that they could not take the risk of another rebellion.

The Council abridged English law and custom to achieve its ends. Repeatedly oversight from England looked the other way. Documents indicate a significant level of discomfort when the vote was taken away from propertied freemen who happened to be black. Virginia Governor Gooch explained the need for such action, concluding that so few people were involved it was hardly worth noticing.

What followed was an extended period in which laws were passed to highlight and increase the distance between whites and Africans of the

---

[37] Allen (1997) p. 239
[38] Ibid, p. 240

laboring-class. To cement the impact of these laws, church wardens were required to read them once each Spring and Fall following a worship service. Sheriffs were required to read them once per year. The net effect, the expansion of acceptance among the people of these decisions that legitimized racialization of society.

Allen reports the Gooch letter as the clearest expression of this process of racialization. In the letter he argued four points

1) Discovery of a plot in 1722 by African-American bond-laborers
2) To make the Free Negros sensible that a distinction ought to be made between their offspring and the descendants of an Englishman
3) To discourage that kind (inter-racial) of copulation, and
4) The persons affected were too few for consideration.[39]

The Gooch letter

> ...gets to the heart of the motives of the Anglo-American continental plantation bourgeoisie in imposing not just a system of lifetime bond-servitude only on persons of African descent, but a system of *racial oppression*, by denying recognition of, refusing to acknowledge, delegitimizing, so far as African-Americans were concerned, the normal social distinctions characteristic of capitalist society.[40] (emphasis in the original)

The times were difficult. The stakes were high. Such a pressure packed time usually reveals the nature and values at work among those involved. The future was not predetermined. The decisions of the past demonstrated a pattern of self-serving by the elites, but they could have

---

[39] Ibid, p. 242
[40] Ibid

charted a different course. The lack of oversight and consequences from England gave decision makers latitude to abridge the rights of residents in the Colony. The decision to racialize the solution to their situation was intentional. We should not be confused. At this moment the leaders of the Colony intentionally enacted a *system of racial oppression* and unknowingly set the course for the nation which followed. This course is defined by a paradox: a nation embracing the lofty values of the Declaration of Independence, life, liberty, and the pursuit of happiness while building its wealth on a system of racial oppression.

Moment Two

In 1987 a celebration was planned in Philadelphia to commemorate the 200th anniversary of the signing of the Constitution of the United States of America. Justice Thurgood Marshall, in an essay published in the Harvard Law Review, explained his unwillingness to participate in the process.

> I cannot accept this invitation, for I do not believe that the meaning of the Constitution was forever "fixed" at the Philadelphia Convention. Nor do I find the wisdom, foresight, and sense of justice exhibited by the framers particularly profound. To the contrary, the government they devised was defective from the start, requiring several amendments, a civil war, and momentous social transformation to attain the system of constitutional government, and its respect for the individual freedoms and human rights, that we hold as fundamental today. When contemporary Americans cite "The Constitution, "they invoke a concept that is vastly different from what the framers barely began to construct two centuries ago.[41]

The discussions and the Convention which produced the Constitution are Moment Two. Marshall, the grandson of a slave and the first African-American to serve on the Supreme Court, expresses his particular perspective which provides commentary on both the convention and the document itself. His essay sent shock waves throughout the legal and political communities. If that wasn't sufficient, Marshall gave a speech to the San Francisco Patent and Trademark Law Association. His theme: "That the Constitution as originally written was profoundly racist.[42] His basis is not found in open references to race or slavery in the document. Rather, it is the clauses that indicate the compromises over slavery that are in the document. Marshall's position is that these three clauses affirm Chief Justice Taney's statement in the Dred Scot case, "the government under the Constitution was of whites, by whites, and for whites only.[43]

<u>Article I, section 2, clause 3</u> reflects the compromise regarding taxation and representation in the House of Representatives. The Articles of Confederation gave states equal voting in Congress. This Constitution needed to satisfy the demands of states with larger populations for more representation. The conundrum, how do you count slaves, not at all or as whole persons? Neither of these options would work. States received equal representation in the Senate and proportional representation in the House. The three-fifths accounting was a compromise using the Confederation basis for taxation which counted slaves as three-fifths of a person for the purpose of taxation. Diamond contends that the compromise induced the South to accept the Constitution because this clause assured it of control over the issue of slavery for some time to come. At the time of the convention it was assumed that population growth in the new country would be in the south and southwest. If this had happened, then the subsequent history of conflict with in the Federal government with debates over new territories would have been mute. The irony of history, population

---

[41] Marshall, pp. 1-2
[42] Diamond, p. 94
[43] Ibid, p. 112

would expand west and northwest.

Article I, section 9, clause 1 "merely prevented Congress from acting to prohibit the African slave trade for a period of twenty years."[44] Positions on this clause are not what you might expect. Virginia wanted to curtail the importation of new slaves from Africa immediately. The had an excess of slaves and did not want competition which drove the price of slaves down. Northern states were ambiguous. They had shipping interests that derived profit from the importation of slaves. Only South Carolina and Georgia pushed against any limit at all. Upper South delegates were most vocal regarding the moral aspects of continuing such a "abominable" and "nefarious trade." Suggestions are that the Prohibition until 1808 while finally enacted did not fully eliminate the importation of Africans. The Northern blockade of Southern seaports would be necessary to enforce the law.

Article IV, section 2, clause 3 is a clear statement of property rights. Slaves are property and that condition cannot be remedied by crossing state lines. This issue was not generally considered significant except for possible bargaining between north and south.

Arguments that the compromises in these clauses were essential to the formation of union are strong. That fact does not remove the Constitution from one of our moments. The political elements of the newly formed states were in process of forming a nation. To form that nation, they had to affirm the processes of racialization. If this price was not too high, we should at least be grateful to those we ask to pay it.

Moment Three

---

[44] Ibid, p. 114

The election of Abraham Lincoln in 1860 precipitated a national crisis. The racialization embodied in slavery was not the sole factor that precipitated this crisis, but it was significant. Moment Three is the election of President Lincoln. This choice is arbitrary due to the continuous presence of racializing behavior and policy making within American history. Lincoln's election changed the racial calculus. Slave states had lost ruling advantage when population moved west and northwest rather than south. The compromises of the last 50 years had provided very little hope that they could extend their economic model. After decades of empty threats to leave the Union, slave states did just that forming the Confederate States of America.

Since before the founding of the nation there had been a persistent background noise of antislavery voices. Abolitionists and some few religious leaders were persistent, their impact limited. Southern economic and political leaders defended slavery as their constitutional and cultural right. For the most part, southern religious leaders developed a framework for biblical interpretation that added legitimacy and contributed to process of racialization in our culture.

On occasion the tensions became public. In addition to undocumented local examples, the Missouri Compromise, the Dred Scott supreme court decision, the Compromise of 1850, and the Kansas-Nebraska Act are a few major examples. In the formation of the Confederacy the threats to the formation of the Union that resulted in the compromises in the Constitution became acts that precipitated a costly Civil War.

Our focus is upon the new tensions arising from the defeat of the Confederacy.

> For a brief period after the Civil War there was a possibility ...(for) a social structure that would allow Southerners, both black and white, to keep more of the value of their own sweat. They might have owned their own bodies and their own labor as well as the land they needed for real freedom. Those who were not farming,

> but selling themselves piecemeal in North and South, would have received higher wages. That this road was not taken is testimony to the power of an elite determined to protect its right to wring as much sweat out of "little guys" as it can get away with. It is equally testimony to the power of racism to blind those who are suffering, so that they support the social structure that causes their pain.[45]

The origins of this 'brief hope' to which Buck refers begins in the summer of 1862. Lincoln was pushing for some form of compensated slave emancipation in the border states, hoping to put an end to the Confederacy's hope that these slave states would join them. Lincoln realized that the cost to purchase all the slaves in border states was less than the cost of the war for 90 days.[46] Bitter and contentious debate in Congress provided no significant solutions. "For Lincoln, the problem of slavery was not an abstract issue. While he concurred with the most passionate abolitionists that slavery was a "'moral, social and a political wrong,"' as president he could not ignore the constitutional protection of the institution where it already existed."[47] By July, Lincoln was considering what would become the Emancipation Proclamation. In December, after his re-election Lincoln's mind is once again on the Proclamation. His fear is that the liberation of the slaves in rebel states would not survive the peace. This explains the push for the Thirteenth Amendment in January of 1865. It had passed the Senate the year before. Now the House had to act before it could be submitted to the states. By December of 1865 it was the newest addition to the Constitution of the United States.

Thirteenth Amendment (1865)

Section 1. Neither slavery nor involuntary servitude, except as a

---

[45] Buck, p.65
[46] Goodwin, p. 459
[47] Ibid, p. 462

punishment for crime whereof the party shall have been duly convicted, shall exist within the United States, or any place subject to their jurisdiction.

Section 2. Congress shall have power to enforce this article by appropriate legislation

Securing the end of slavery could not be the final act. By 1865 the racialization of the United States had taken on an even more sinister program. On August 14, 1862, President Lincoln met with a delegation of freed slaves. His hope for the meeting was to persuade them to support efforts for either sending freed slaves to Liberia or establishing an additional colony for them in Africa. After acknowledging that slave experience was "the greatest wrong inflicted on any people," the President summarized the effect of racialized behavior

> You and we are different races. We have between us a broader difference than exists between almost any other two races. When you cease to be slaves, you are yet far removed from being placed on an equality with the white race. You are cut off from many of the advantages which the other race enjoy. The aspiration of men is to enjoy equality with the best when free, but on this broad continent, not a single man of your race is made the equal of a single man of ours.[48]

Lincoln knew that the peace would be hard to win. The removal of the status of slave was not going to remedy the racialized nature of relations in the United States. After his death and during the Reconstruction Period, the Fourteenth and Fifteenth Amendments were efforts to address these deficits. Lincoln's legacy lived in those who first attempted to administer the years after the Civil War. Note the structural changes and the expanded legitimacies incorporated into these amendments. The effort is the brief moment of hope.

---

[48] Ibid, p. 469

Lincoln's understanding of the extent of racialized values and objectives takes shape in Southern response to the Thirteenth Amendment. Black Codes that restricted the freed slaves were passed in 1865 and 1866. These Codes limited the freedom that came with emancipation. The Codes restricted voting and required African-Americans to jobs that were no improvement over slavery. The Codes even restricted the rights to worship, public education, and assembly.

Soon to follow at the federal level were the Civil Rights Acts of 1866, 1871, and 1875. The Fourteenth and Fifteenth Amendments again addressed the issues raised by Taney in the Dred Scott case. The Constitution now established a status of equality. The problem is the implementation of these laws and amendments. As Lincoln knew, racialization was a more intrenched aspect of American Life than legislation could fix.

Fourteenth Amendment (1868)

Section 1. All persons born or naturalized in the United States, and subject to the jurisdiction thereof, are citizens of the United States and of the State wherein they reside. No State shall make or enforce any law which shall abridge the privileges or immunities of citizens of the United States; nor shall any State deprive any person of life, liberty, or property, without due process of law; nor deny to any person within its jurisdiction the equal protection of the laws.

Section 2. Representatives shall be apportioned among the several States according to their respective numbers, counting the whole number of persons in each State, excluding Indians not taxed. But when the right to vote at any election for the choice of electors for President and Vice President of the United States, Representatives in Congress, the Executive and Judicial officers of a State, or the members of the Legislature thereof, is denied to any of the male inhabitants of such State, being twenty-one years of age, and citizens of the United States, or in any way abridged, except for participation in rebellion, or other crime, the basis of representation therein shall be reduced in the proportion which the number of such male citizens shall bear to the whole number of male citizens twenty-one years of age in such State.

Section 3. No person shall be a Senator or Representative in Congress, or elector of President and Vice President, or hold any office, civil or military, under the United States, or under any State, who, having previously taken an oath, as a member of Congress, or as an officer of the United States, or as a member of any State legislature, or as an executive or judicial officer of any State, to support the Constitution of the United States, shall have engaged in insurrection or rebellion against the same, or given aid or comfort to the enemies thereof. But Congress may, by a vote of two-thirds of each House, remove such disability.

Section 4. The validity of the public debt of the United States, authorized by law, including debts incurred for payment of pensions and bounties for services in suppressing insurrection or rebellion, shall not be questioned. But neither the United States nor any State shall assume or pay any debt or obligation incurred in aid of insurrection or rebellion against the United States, or any claim for the loss or emancipation of any slave; but all such debts, obligations and claims shall be held illegal and void.

Section 5. The Congress shall have power to enforce, by appropriate legislation, the provisions of this article.

Fifteenth Amendment (1870)

Section 1. The right of citizens of the United States to vote shall not be denied or abridged by the United States or by any State on account of race, color, or previous condition of servitude.

Section 2. The Congress shall have power to enforce this article by appropriate legislation.

A series of five cases, known as the Civil Rights Cases, came before the

Supreme Court. These cases were an indirect attempt by the southern establishment to nullify the Thirteenth, Fourteenth, and Fifteenth Amendments. Where the Black Codes were direct challenges on the basis of race, the Civil Rights Cases were cloaked in the issues of states' rights.

Buck's assessment of the Kentucky experience applies across the south.

> After the Civil War local Southern elites continued to preside over the new system at the local level, but they were more tightly tied into the national drainage system. They were utterly dependent on the ideology of white supremacy and the psychological wage to maintain control of the Blacks and Whites whose sweat they drained. They played on white fears of black reprisals for slavery, and on the unsupported fear that black men would start raping white women just as generations of white men had raped black women. Most southern Whites, regardless of class, readily agreed that Blacks were dangerous, and that they wouldn't work except when forced. The legal divisions of free or enslaved had disappeared with emancipation, leaving the now widely accepted belief in the biological reality of race to bear the entire burden of making these claims appear plausible.[49]

Whiteness is morphing. The challenges created by altering the legal structure of the country proved to be inadequate in the face of racialization. The passing of Black Codes in Ohio, Illinois, Michigan, New York, and Indiana revealed the extent to which racialization had become a national habit. As late as 1890 90% of African-Americans lived in the rural South. From 1890 to 1970 as many as 6 million African-Americans moved to the norther parts of the country which left 53% of African-Americans living in the South, but now more frequently in urban areas.

---

[49] Buck, p. 65

Most of migrants settled in northern cities as well.

The Supreme Court accepted the supremacy of states' rights over the newly minted citizens rights for African-Americans. Their rejection of the Civil Rights Acts as the congressional prerogative to legislate the administration of changes framed by the new amendments left the door open for individual states to initiate what became known as the Jim Crow laws. One voice of dissent from the Supreme Court is worthy of citation.

> I do not contend that the thirteenth amendment invests congress with authority, by legislation, to regulate the entire body of the civil rights which citizens enjoy, or may enjoy, in the several states. But I do hold that since slavery, as the court has repeatedly declared, was the moving or principal cause of the adoption of that amendment, and since that institution rested wholly upon the inferiority, as a race, of those held in bondage, their freedom necessarily involved immunity from, and protection against, all discrimination against them, because of their race, in respect of such civil rights as belong to freemen of other races. Congress, therefore, under its express power to enforce that amendment, by appropriate legislation, may enact laws to protect that people against the deprivation, on account of their race, of any civil rights enjoyed by other freemen in the same state; and such legislation may be of a direct and primary character, operating upon states, their officers and agents, and also upon, at least, such individuals and corporations as exercise public functions and wield power and authority under the state.[50]

Jim Crow characterized the racialization habit for more than 80 years. Separate but equal became its public face. Separate and unequal

---

[50] Justice John Harlan, Dissent position Civil Rights Cases

remained its reality. The violence imposed by slave owners to maintain their position was replaced by the open violence of the Ku Klux Klan and other mobs, particularly in lynching, to terrorized freed African-American citizens. Jim Crow's reign of terror was used to enforce the caste system in its new formation. Legal niceties did not overcome culture. The culture of the United States during Jim Crow was hardly changed from that of slavery. African-Americans and White Americans occupied two different life-worlds.

Moment Four

The Civil Rights Movement took modern shape as World War II was coming to an end. In record numbers African-Americans fought in the Armed Forces of the United States. That is true of every American war, the difference, the deconstruction of the colonial world which became an identifiable contrast to how African-Americans fared in the United States. The Universal Declaration of Human Rights in 1948 illuminated our cultural hypocrisy in maintaining a habit of racializing society.

I cannot document all aspects of this moment. The attack on Jim Crow. The work in the Warren Court that fundamentally changed the states' rights advantage. The Civil Rights Act of 1964 and the Voting Rights Act of 1965 delegitimized Jim Crow. The legal battle to secure these rights is not complete as of July 2018.

Addressing desegregation in schools, neighborhoods, unions, and churches is more than a legal battle, it is a cultural change of habits. Consider the words of Sears *et al*

> Race relations in the United States have had a long history, but one that is marked by significant discontinuities over time. The period of slavery was followed by the brief but radically different window of

Reconstruction. The Jim crow system that developed over the following century legalized racial segregation and discrimination, especially but not exclusively in the South. The civil rights revolution effectively ended the two caste system of race relations, replacing it with a universal system of formal legal equality. Nevertheless, considerable racial inequality remains in many areas of the society, such as in income, wealth, educational attainment, health, crime, and so forth.

The demise of Jim Crow was accompanied by a sharp decline in the prevalence of it supporting belief system. This has been described as "'old-fashioned racism,'" incorporating both a biologically based theory of African racial inferiority and support for racial segregation...there is much evidence that whites do not fully support the implications of these general principles of equality.[51]

One of the reasons that whiteness is able to morph at each of the moments we noted is summed up in the statement above, 'civil rights revolution effectively ended the two caste system of race relations, replacing it with a universal system of formal legal equality' which declares victory far too quickly. Granted, the legitimacy of Jim Crow was removed. The culture that sustained Jim Crow, a national culture, was undermined but has not disappeared. Overt expressions of racialization have been and generally are sanctioned. The generations since 1965 have experienced more challenges to white supremacy. In fact most whites think the problem is now fabricated to give unfair advantage to people of color. This is supported by the last statement in the quote above, "much evidence that whites do not fully support the implications of these general principles of equality." The policy attempts to alter the cultural aspects of our national habit of racialization have generally met with tepid support. Mention quotas or affirmative action and the

---

[51] Sears *et al*, pp. 16-17

support from whites for these policies does not match declarations of believing in the equality of all. Rather, commitments are to race-neutrality or color-blindness.

When white habits become illegal expect them to discover a new form. We considered in light of Giddens' motivations for action, agents have both conscious and unconscious motivations. De-legitimation or making something illegal may have a much greater impact on what is conscious. The implicit biases of white elites, making laws or hiring employees, if left unchallenged could become the new Jim Crow.

Consider the legislation on sentencing related to the war on drugs. Possessing 5 grams of crack cocaine carries a minimum sentence of 5 years. Possessing the same quantity of powder cocaine is a misdemeanor with jail time of less than one year. Is it a surprise that crack is the drug of choice in African-American communities, while powder is preferred by whites? Is this intentional or implicit? If you are convicted possessing crack cocaine it does not matter. Either way it is tolerated by the unchallenged acceptance of the devaluing and dehumanizing characterization of African-Americans.

The war on drugs has not been won. It has mired our country in counter-productive battles. Why can we not win this war? The following details one consequence of this period for American communities. We incarcerate more citizens than any other industrial country. They are disproportionately African-American. Our national acceptance is reflection of implicit bias.

> The U.S. penal population increased six fold between 1972 and 2000, leaving 1.3 million men in state and federal prisons by the end of the century. By 2002, around 12 percent of black men in their twenties were in prison or jail (Harrison and Karberg 2003). High incarceration rates led researchers to claim that prison time had become a part of the early adulthood for black men in poor urban neighborhoods (Freeman 1996;

Irwin and Austin 1997). In this period of mass imprisonment, it was argued, official criminality attached not just to individual offenders, but to whole social groups defined by their race, age, and class (Garland 2001a:2).[52]

A final point, the challenge on racialization in the 1960s has forced a new face on whiteness. For all of our history white has been normal. If the cultural conversations since the civil rights movement has made whiteness less defensible, the elites are forced to redefine themselves. Whiteness has hidden behind the concept of meritocracy. Theoretically a meritocracy allows the best to rise to the top. The problem with this concept is that it fits so well with American mythology of the strong individual. The challenge to the utilization of merit for social promotion is the assumption that everyone starts from the same place. God may create us as equal, our culture has us sorted by the time we leave the hospital. The caste system may be weaker today than earlier in our history, but I question whether it remains in our cultural subconscious.

If whiteness finds a way to morph with every challenge, how do we ever achieve the American goal of equality?

---

[52] Petit, p. 151

6 OUR STRUGGLE: POWER/PRINCIPALITIES

*For struggle is not against enemies of blood and flesh,
but against the rulers, against the authorities, against
the cosmic powers of this present darkness, against the
spiritual forces of evil in the heavenly places. (Ep. 6: 12)
NRSV*

Steps to reduce the racialized character of the U.S. society have only achieved partial success. Why? Political and economic efforts have not reversed what these same processes initiated in Virginia at the hands of the Colonial Council. The force employed to destroy the racialized order during the Civil War is no match for the force used since 1676 to terrorize and cement the racialized order. At the few junctures where success was achieved it has faced reversals and erosion.

In this chapter I develop an appraisal to this problem which draws from philosophical, sociological, and theological sources. The social (political and economic) response to Bacon's Rebellion set in motion processes more consequential than those decision makers could have imagined. The unintended consequences of their actions were a two-caste society that required a reorientation of many aspects of the British life-world to justify and maintain the change. Individuals were required to see a 'new reality:' being white as the normative status for full membership in society. Social habits would alter to align with this 'new reality.'

Such a change is possible within a society only if it can be legitimized. Legitimization allows the new to become an alternative on its way to becoming the norm. Science was used to support a theory of essential differences establishing white superiority. The same is true of cultural differences. But more was needed. Theology provided ultimate legitimization: Africans are less than human because of God's created order or the curse of Ham, or other lines of argument current in sermons and teaching since that time.

The two-caste society was the physical manifestation of these efforts, but what about an inner change? Did the taken-for-granted connections between members of the society change? I am convinced they did. Did all of these actions and justifications alter the internal state of members of the society? I am convinced it did. Did the spiritual world of these members change? It did and I am convinced that the explanation for the tenacity of whiteness initiated racialization is located in these issues!

As a Follower of Jesus, I appreciate the challenges climate sciences face. Their experience and knowledge are questioned by those who refuse to interpret climate data following their models. The models I follow for a spiritual assessment of whiteness are challengeable. Doubters are warned. I will develop an analysis of the spiritual implications of whiteness from both my religious and sociological training, informed by my experience.

Walter Wink has developed the most comprehensive framework for our analysis. His multiple volume work on the powers discussed in the New Testament provides both the categories and much of the language for a discussion on the spiritual implications of whiteness. The challenge to any such discussion begins with language.

For more than fifty years, I have provided some level of leadership within various Christian communities. In this area I have received training at the master's level. Yet, when I sat down to begin this section I have struggled to define spiritual and spirituality. When looking for a definition I found that most sources provide circular definitions, employing some form of the concept in the definition.

Wink begins

> "Spiritual" here means the inner dimension of the material, the within of things, the subjectivity of objective entities in the world. Instead of the old dualism of matter and spirit, we can now regard matter and spirit as united in one indivisible reality, distinguishing in two discrete but interrelated manifestations.[53]

A simple, straight forward, and unsatisfying definition. The spiritual is the inner aspects of material realities. While my western perspective holds the pantheistic implications of this definition suspect, his application across the social presents an interesting and engaging perspective.

The interior of mankind would be the soul. Nothing new here. Wink argues that the spiritual beings and dimensions of power present in the biblical worldview represent this interiority. Angels and demons are first century depictions of the interiority of communities and organizations. Powers and principalities are the spiritual aspects of collective behavior. An angel would be associated with a particular social reality. Most surprisingly, Wink asserts a reflexive relationship between the material and spiritual. When national life demonstrates righteousness, then the angel of that nation reinforces the good. Where the nation acts in evil ways, the angel moves towards the demonic. Each state of being real, each impacting the other.

Wink's work intrigued me. He engages a hermeneutic process to bring a First Century mythic worldview into a 20th Century conceptual world. I found it interesting but wondered where I would find it applicable.

---

[53] Wink vol 1 p. 107

Early sociologists struggled with the subjective aspects of society. Max Weber worked to document the subjective meaning of social behavior. Emile Durkheim wrote extensively about the moral aspects of social life. Anthony Giddens has used the work of a philosopher, Edmund Husserl, to structure his social theory.

For more than 30 years Husserl's project of explaining human existence centered on intersubjectivity as "constitutive of the Subject and the very notion of an objective world."[54] Duranti uses an extended quote from Schutz to demonstrate Husserl's focus on intersubjectivity.

> [*Intersubjectivity*] is the fundamental ontological
> category of human existence in the world and therefore
> of all philosophical anthropology. As long as man is born
> of woman, intersubjectivity and the we-relationship will
> be the foundation for all other categories of human
> existence. The possibility of reflection on the self,
> discovery of the ego, capacity for performing any
> epoché, and the possibility of all communication and of
> establishing a communicative surrounding world as
> well, are founded on the primal experience of the we-
> relationship. (Schutz, 1966: 82) [Italics in original.]

Intersubjectivity is a theoretical issue for Husserl explaining the possibility for meaningful human action. He proposes intersubjectivity as the condition which makes that meaningful action possible within defined human communities. Being unable to observe the origins of human community we are restricted to the re-formation of society. Other people evoke this 'we-relationship.' The evidence of the 'we-relationship' can be taken from the products of social life.

Duranti builds a propositional case for integrated anthropological study from the explication of intersubjectivity.

---

[54] Duranti p. 1

1. The experience of the natural world, which by being shared, already constitutes a 'form of community'.
2. The experience of the world as apprehended through the senses, which, in the 'natural attitude', are always in combination with our empathetic co-presence with other living bodies, whose actions reveal their intentions…
3. The experience of the natural world as a world through which human presence and human labor has already been transformed into a 'cultural world…the world of 'places' as opposed to 'spaces'…
4. The participation in a world inhabited by Others, always perceived and understood as particular types of beings…
5. The being-with of specific encounters, interactions, joint activities, in the present as well as in the remembered past and in the anticipated future…(is a) world of 'doing together' … a pragmatic world, that is, a world constituted by our actions and made sense through them.
6. We need to become aware of the fact that language displays and invokes intersubjectivity even before it can be decoded according to grammatical or lexical information.[55]

Intersubjectivity and spirituality both describe the capacity for a connection to another or other Beings. Researching both leads me to conclude a haunting similarity of the effort to define and describe a condition that appears necessary to those who propose and utilize their respective concepts to account for the gaps encountered as they attempt to explain human life and community. Spirituality may or may not presuppose a divine or supernatural order. Intersubjectivity presupposes nothing of the kind.

Wink is painstaking to describe powers in the New Testament as both human and divine. Do not read this as human or divine. He states that the New Testament authors and the Apostle Paul in particular are using the mythic world view and its language to describe the presence of good and evil in the world. The assumption is that all powers were

---

[55] Ibid, pp. 11-13

created by God to serve the purpose of God to structure an existence for mankind characterized by *shalom*. The brokenness and evil in the world is the consequences of resentment and rebellion to this purpose.

> Every Power tends to have a visible pole, an outer form—be it a church, a nation, or an economy—and an invisible pole, an inner spirit or driving force that animates, legitimates, and regulates it physical manifestation in the world. Neither pole is the cause of the other. Both come into existence together and cease to exist together. When a particular Power becomes idolatrous placing itself above God's purposes for the good of the whole, that that Power becomes demonic.[56]

Hear Paul express a rather significant level of intersubjectivity.

> ...for in him all things in heaven and on earth were created, things visible and invisible, whether thrones or dominions or rulers or powers—all things have been created through him and for him. He himself is before all things, and in him all things hold together. (Colossians 1: 16-17) NRSV

Wink's presentation on spirituality through his work on Powers in the New Testament supports this analytical framework. Creation established a Divine purpose (*shalom*) for humans and all of the created order. Idolatrous tendencies and forces have subverted aspects of the creation to work against God's purpose. At the center of this process is the power struggle which reveals the allegiance of all parties.

In the face of more than 300 years within a racialized society, in which multiple attempts to de-racialize have failed, our analysis must reckon with the evidence that personal and national habits persist despite efforts to change. Recent years reveal our progress and the fact that progress is too slow for those who remain trapped by a social system

---

[56] Wink vol 1, p. 5

that devalues them and their participation. There are members of our society who do not see whiteness as a social habit. For them race is an essential element in the world. I am the product of family lines with such a worldview. I have had my own struggles with racialization, none of them reaching the level of white supremacy, but clearly whiteness defined by implicit bias. The struggle within my family reflects the national struggle.

For the essentialists among us this is an issue of worldview. Their world is constructed by clear categories structured by naturally occurring characteristics. Clearly, I do not agree with a definition of race that draws upon naturally occurring factors, it is a construction of our social life. Can you expect people who do not see a problem to address it? We cannot. Public action, such as the passage of law and the amending of the constitution may remove the legitimizing supports for the habit of racialization, but the essentialists will define such efforts as misguided or even messing with the natural order.

Buck's position is that our national habit is an intentional pattern promoted by the economic and political elites at local and national levels. They perpetuate the caste system to avoid the challenges of class conflict. She believes that class conflict would be more destabilizing to the interests of the elites. To the degree she is correct, this makes the national habit fraud which promotes the interest of a few. I know of no other characterization for this than evil.

While I reject the essentialist position and have more than a sympathetic ear for the elite fraud position, my sociological and theological perspectives indicate that our national habit of racializing is more complicated. The historical material we have considered indicates the times when elites did engage propaganda campaigns to promote racialization for their benefits. This does not explain the depth to which racialization engaged my family and our society. Race based interaction is a fact because millions of white US citizens engage one or more of the three types of whiteness.

The continual practice of whiteness is dependent upon its daily utilization in our society. I would refer you to the Model of Agent Stratification developed by Anthony Giddens to depict agency in humans. Whiteness which is unacknowledged is part of our unconscious motivations of action. African-Americans, because of their history with all expressions of whiteness, recognize the elements of whiteness as they encounter them.   We shouldn't be surprised by the lack of awareness among whites because whiteness is our culture.

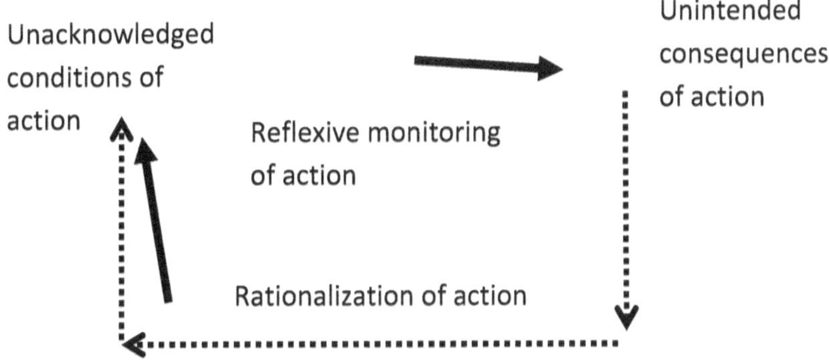

Gidden's Model for Agent Stratification of Action

As early (or recent depending on your perspective) academic articles by white scholars on whiteness began to appear[57] the dominate theme was awareness or self-awareness. They were surprised by their whiteness. As I have discussed the theme of this book with various contacts, friends, family, and colleagues, I have heard more than a few relate a similar process. To a person, all were surprised. What scholars and golfing buddies alike demonstrate is the power of culture.

We whites are frequently taken by surprise by the cultural origins of our separateness and that this contributes to a caste stratified society which itself is the result of that whiteness. This is a level of awareness that is

---

[57] McIntosh 1988

not part of our daily awareness as white Americans. This lack of awareness demonstrates the different life worlds into which we are socialized and where our personalities are formed. These life worlds are social environments where the routine nature of daily life is not generally noticed. The sheer number of demands placed upon a human require our ability to develop routines that free us for demands less routine. Culture is the mechanism through which these routine behavior and attitudes are made available to members of a society.

Giddens' Agent Stratification models the innerworkings of individuals in society.[58] His theoretical approach to the agency of individuals describes three aspects of an individual that are similar to but different from Freud's *id*, *ego*, and *super-ego*. Giddens characterizes the agent as constructed by three interacting aspects: <u>basic security system</u>, <u>practical consciousness</u>, and <u>discursive consciousness</u>.

The <u>basic security system</u> of an individual develops within social contacts that begin with parents and expand outward. We need to learn that our needs will be met and that we are safe. We begin to learn this before we can form or understand verbal communication. Our interactions beginning in infancy establish patterns of anxiety and trust. Trust is developed with those who are consistently 'with' us. This is the reason that we are 'socialized' into the life world of our parents. The consistent physical presence of parents and family allow for routines to develop and become a part of the life of the child. More should be said on this process. My aim is to establish the connection between these early experiences and the process of agents to develop basic security systems which form the basis of our unconscious. The unconsciousness is the location for the numerous motives for action for which we have no explanation.

I suggest that much of our whiteness that can be found, if that were possible, in our unconsciousness. The messaging which began with the Virginia Colonial Council intending to disrupt the life worlds of African

---

[58] Giddens (1984) pp. 41-109

bond-laborers and English bond-laborers by establishing Africans as violent and evil had its intended impact. The persistent non-rational fear of black males demonstrates unmotivated action. Why would I locate this fear in our collective white unconsciousness, the socialization of multiple generations of white infants in families like mine since 1750?

Agents are located in social systems. Social systems are regularized social practices. Agents experience those practices based on their position in the society. What is regularized in our experience becomes 'normal.' When social practices are established as normal they become routine. Sociologists designate this process by the term, routinization. Agents develop or acquire <u>practical consciousness</u> which facilitates negotiating what is routine with the greatest efficiency. In this way the routine processes of a society are 'stored' with agents, to use and to pass on to the next generation. These routines are changeable. They are social constructions that can change. But, consider the magnitude of such change in a society of 300,000,000+ agents.

Having been socialized by agents reared in the American caste system, white American agents have routines that they utilize without critical examination. Such examination is possible but requires some intervention that calls the routine into question. This happened to me when my use of the term 'jewing' was called into question. Whiteness at this level provides a roadmap for negotiating life. It is a map that we follow without notice until that intervention which brings the map into focus. We can explain the map only at these times.

Here is a critical juncture for change. What happens when whites become aware of the map of caste relations in America? It depends. I know, not such a profound answer, but as honest an answer as I have. When the intervention makes you aware of your whiteness, how prepared are you to face this realization? Are you making this realization in an environment that either supports or is hostile to the perception of whiteness? In short, where are you located and in what social network are you becoming aware?

Agents monitor their actions and the actions of others, that reflexive monitoring of action is contingent on our level of <u>discursive consciousness</u>. A white 20-year-old male in a social network that has not perceived the social basis of race is exposed to a discursive consciousness that is a very different set of factors than someone situated in a network that is open to such a discussion. Do these two hypothetical white males have different realities? No, but they do have radically different sets of social knowledge which structures their practical and discursive consciousness.

In this way social change is uneven. This discussion of agency and change is very truncated. You have multiple resources available as easily as google scholar or picking up a copy of Giddens' *The Constitution of Society*. Culture is largely practices of which we are not aware because we do not often question what we consider normal. We whites are not aware of whiteness because we consider it normal, it is our culture. We should not be surprised that we are surprised by the perception of our whiteness. The question then becomes our ability to take responsibility for its manifestations and its outcomes.

From the vantage point of my late 60s, I am able to look back at the various perceptions that impacted the monitoring I did of social action. I see their cumulative impact. I grudgingly acknowledge my resistance to the knowledge that I was impacted by racializing messages from my family and culture. I was too optimistic and often unrealistic to the level of change occurring. I was baffled by the complaints in the 70s and 80s that things were not that much better for African-Americans. It took becoming the father of an African-American daughter; living in inner-city North St. Louis in a public housing complex for 5 years as an urban missionary; contending with African-American university students who were struggling with their community as they tried to pursue higher education; and teaching African-American students in a small town whose life had been turned upside-down by the degree of whiteness in the culture of the town and the Christian educational institution where they studied.

This Christian institution of higher education has the best intentions. It is serious about extending the teachings of Jesus at its campus and around the world. Realizing the make-up of their student body, it has taken steps to welcome people of color as part of their commitment to living the Gospel in a diverse world. It intentionally sought and employed a racially diverse faculty. The board of trustees was equally diversified. Yet people of color who participate, faculty and students, experience a disconnect between the intentions and the lived realities. Why has an institution committed to such high values failed?

Like so many whites who are sympathetic to the plight of the 'other' and who expend considerable resources to 'make a difference,' they miss an accurate perception of racialization. While focused on the margins of our social stratification map, leaders of this institution fail to see that it is whiteness that creates the 'other.' When challenged to address the white history of the institution and the situated whiteness that perpetuates the implicit bias that people of color experience, leaders respond with surprise that their efforts are being rebuffed by either ungrateful people or they are victims of 'reverse racism.'

Why is 'white constructed identity' a continual stumbling stone for even those whites who seriously commit themselves to ending racism?

White constructed identity is a cultural characteristic that hides in plain sight. This aspect of culture is as resistant to change as any other. The transmutation of protests initiated by black athletes targeting police killings of unarmed African-Americans into an unpatriotic act that is offensive to military veterans is a recent example of the tenacity of culture. Merely developing a sociological frame for analyzing whiteness does not change the monitoring of action. The significant steps forward to overt racism in diminished prejudice and segregation may only intensify the elements of racialization that remain.

I turn now to a tool available for analyzing and addressing issues of white constructed identity that creates a social stratification system that severely disadvantages those who are not considered white. My own discipline of sociology is often hostile to this tool and has contributed to the demise of religion and the disappearance of God from social equations.

Do you hear someone struggling with the reflexive monitoring of their action or struggling with the unintended consequences of their action in these words?

> For we know that the law is spiritual; but I am of the flesh, sold into slavery under sin. I do not understand my own actions. For I do not do what I want, but I do the very thing I hate. Now if I do what I do not want, I agree that the law is good. But in fact it is no longer I that do it, but sin that dwells within me. For I know that nothing good dwells within me, that is, in my flesh. I can will what is right, but I cannot do it. For I do not do the good I want, but the evil I do not want is what I do. Now if I do what I do not want, it is no longer I that do it, but sin that dwells within me.

> So I find it to be a law that when I want to do what is good, evil lies close at hand. For I delight in the law of god in my inmost self, but I see in my members another law at war with the law of my mind, making me captive to the law of sin that dwells in my members. Wretched man that I am! Who will rescue me from this body of death? Thanks be to God through Jesus Christ our Lord.

> So then, with my mind I am a slave to the law of God, but with my flesh I am a slave to the law of sin. (Rom. 7: 14-25) NRSV

At first glance, Paul's words baffle a modern approach to the struggles of mankind. We cannot understand easily a mythic approach to ourselves and our world. In Paul's perspective the barrier between the unconscious and the discursive consciousness he desires exerts undesired impacts on his behavior. He is aware of the expectations brought to his life by the law of God. He is equally aware of the situated resistance to those expectations by forces at work within him. He categorizes those forces as 'flesh.' In these verses Paul expresses a reflexive process in which he is reconciling the acceptance in theory of an outside (law of God) perception upon his unexplained motivations for action.

In the same mythic language, the characteristic of culture discussed above where collective habits are stored with individuals and become visible when agents pursue their goals is available to Paul.

> For our struggle is not against enemies of blood and flesh, but against the rulers, against the authorities, against the cosmic powers of this present darkness, against the spiritual forces of evil in the heavenly places. (Ep. 6: 12) NRSV

Paul is a messenger engaged in social and cultural change. He is communicating a message that has developed from his vision of Jesus on the road from Damascus and his Jewish education. Paul's message explains how God has entrusted the reconciliation between Himself and a rebellious and broken world. Reconciliation results in a world characterized by *shalom*, the well-being of all creation. In such a world well-being is not a zero-sum game. Well-being for some is never purchased by the disadvantage of others.

The struggle to which Paul refers stands against those forces who oppose the reconciliation program of God. This passage indicates that these forces are encountered as human and the suprahuman. The battleground is both earthly and heavenly. Wink interprets this "heaping up of terms to describe the ineffable, invisible world-enveloping reach of a spiritual network of powers inimical to life."[59]

In earlier chapters we have seen that the English who came to Virginia

---

[59] Wink vol 1, p. 85

came as cultural products / producers. In pursuit of their goals they replicated and modified the cultural habits imported to America. Our analysis is straightforward yet complex: do the habits they established harm we-relationships (intersubjectivity) or promote *shalom* (biblical *shalom*)?

If intersubjectivity is an *a priori* concept speaking to human social potential and *shalom* is the conceptual expression of realized human potential, then together they pose the complex empirical questions. What habits comprise each? What habits strengthen each?

The we-relationship of intersubjectivity benefits from face to face relationships that are generalized to the population at large. Members of a society that value the common bonds of their connection increase the operational presence of we-relationship. Mutual understanding requires open and honest communication. The association of we-relationship with empathy is high. Empathetic relationships allow people to 'trade places' or to comprehend the life of another. The connection created allows the other person to be a distinct being with equal rights and standing. The conditions allow for extensive potential in the relationships. Putnam would find many of these characteristics in the concept of social capital.

Spiritual life is lived to honor and serve a truth or a being larger than one's self. The biblical record describes these characteristics as

- righteousness, living in responsible relationship with others
- compassion, an active acceptance of others finding ways to work through their brokenness, particularly when it impacts you
- worship, recognizing that God is the source of all life which motivates you to gather with others to celebrate the gift of His self-revelation.

Wink takes a Max Weber approach to these questions.[60] The list of behaviors he details is an 'ideal-type' which I will utilize for analytical

---

[60] Wink vol 3, p. 46-47

purposes. I will select several characteristics which illustrate the impact on we-relationship and *shalom*. For clarity I will refer to opposing process as constructive or destructive.

Relationships between social groups in a complex society will become stratified. Consistently this process is determinative of who has access to social goods. Biblical material, particularly Leviticus 25 and Deuteronomy 15, recognize this process. To the degree that stratification limits members from a life promoting level of goods it is tyrannical and destructive. The biblical principle of forgiveness—both of debts and sins—enables a process through which no one should become consistently disadvantaged. Modern societies have experimented with various social safety net models.

Where stratification promotes disadvantage, other societal factors tend towards destructive patterns. As societies have become more complex economic systems have increasingly served elite groups. Economic activity becomes independent of the greater social good.

A similar threat is seen in the political realm. When decisions promote the interests of a few over the greater good another destructive pattern develops.

The continual opting for destructive choices creates a cultural pattern that is stored in its members. It is stored in their unconscious. These patterns perpetuate destructive choices as unacknowledged conditions of action.

The failure to address the spiritual dimensions results in a society described most accurately by the Apostle Paul's words: what I would do, I do not.

The spiritual costs from 300+ years of tolerating a racialized society.

1. We are a people of diminished empathy.
2. We are a society divided into multiple systems of we / them.
3. Self-serving behavior is common; sacrificial behavior is rare.

4. Small tyrannies rather than co-operation characterize our politics and economic lives.
5. To the degree that we ever were a 'Christian nation' it was a representation lacking significant application of tenets Jesus gave us.

The remedy, if we choose, is a spiritual one, repentance. Repentance will require a national conversation that elevates the racialized elements of our unconscious so that we recognize them at the level of motivation for action. We will need to come to terms with those motives and how they have unraveled previous steps towards de-racializing. We will need to submit to reviving we-relationship as foundational to social processes. We will have to lay claim to the aspirational challenge of shalom. Our pride, both personal and national, is likely to prevent any change that will meaningfully challenge whiteness as a foundation for a racialized society.

In American Christianity we have lost the cosmic implications of Jesus' ministry. We ignore and compromise the implications of his temptation. We personalize his crucifixion. We do not give testimony to the new people and the new fellowship he launched. Sure, there are pockets of believers who belie my statements, they are a minority. The history of my family speaks into this issue. For the most part we obeyed the law. Many of us actively participated in organized Christianity. A number of us served as clergy and missionaries. We fought in wars, served as law enforcement. None of that erases our participation in American idolatry. We lived and supported 'whiteness' the ultimate American contribution to the *kosmos*. We supported a pattern of behavior that undermined the focal point of Jesus' ministry. Our 'whiteness' denied a we-relationship to others. Extending we-relationship to the excluded was the reason Jesus command that we daily take up our crosses. We failed!

93

AFTERWARD

Shiloh, Illinois

September 2018

Dear Alec, Brittany, Ally, Justin, Kyla, Landon, Payton, Micah, Autumn, Aiden, Brooks, and Evan (and others to follow):

You are the main reason I wrote this book. Others may read it and if so, I hope it is of some benefit, you are my motivation to think and write. My hope is that you are people who are reflective, that is who monitor your actions and adapt them to improve what you do. I hope that you look below the surface for facts and ask great questions.

You are a member of a special family. Decisions Grandma and I made, not always knowing the full outcome; have set the tone and foundation for us. Your parents and aunts and uncles have filled in the blanks, added to the promise, and extended our commitments. Most of all we are indebted to Grandma. You will never meet another person whose life has been devoted more to others. I had the good sense to follow her lead. She gave and gives to you a life of service and sacrifice from which you have greatly benefited and provides an example of how you are to pass on these benefits to others. You can honor her by folding these actions into your lives.

I have tried to be honest in this book. You will find my blind spots and be amazed that I did not see and understand more. Half of you are people of color, half of you are white, collectively you have ancestors from Africa, Korea, Sweden, Scotland, Ireland, England, the Cherokee nation, and other places yet to be identified. I cannot represent all of these origins. Most of my ancestors are from the British Isles, so I am white. You have only known me as an old white man, hopefully I am not typical of this species.

You know better than I that you live in a world where what you look like sets limits on your living as much or more than any other factor. I have tried in this book to detail some of those other factors. A word of caution to those of you who are white, we cannot accurately judge if the wall between the social life worlds which challenge our family is coming down or getting more porous. Listen to your non-white cousins, their voices will provide the insight you need. Remember...

Our history has created a society deeply divided into two unequal life-worlds. This division runs deep. It is so deep in our lives that it motivates our actions in ways that we do not consciously will or understand. But you must gain this level of awareness. To bridge the potential life-worlds facing you, there must be deep and honest communication. You are equipped to participate in this conversation. Attempt to assist others to become equipped.

The future is uncertain, as of now there is not much public support for an honest conversation. Many white people will not participate because of the central premise of this book: it is whiteness that racializes our society. I trust reading this book has opened you to this idea. I believe there are well-meaning whites who honestly cannot see this situation. I do not know how to help them. If they are too uncertain to open themselves to the possibility this limits our hope. Other whites are openly threatened by an honest conversation, so they hide behind their own declaration of superiority if they are openly racists. They claim no responsibility if they refuse to face the facts of our history. Either are dangerous to your future. But so are the whites who cannot see the role of whiteness. They, too, contribute to division.

I can only speak as an old white man. You grandchildren of mine who have African and Korean ancestors can contribute to the conversation. Find your voice, know your facts, be as honest as you can be.

Very few politicians will help you in this conversation. Very few businessmen will help you. Sadly, very few church leaders will help you. America is captive to self-interest. Today's pragmatism tells us to care for ourselves. I believe pragmatism on behalf of our nation would challenge us to consider what is best for the whole of society. It was business men who controlled the political machinery of Virginia who set in motion this curse that will not be satisfied. Today we have the same situation only with richer business interests and more entrenched political interests. An ethicist named Walzer wrote that it is tyrannical for those who hold a monopoly in one social good (business for example) to exchange that good for advantage in another. Know that the argument that money is speech is not the only legitimate argument regarding the tyranny of their reach in political influence. Our system was established on the basis of voting as participation. Buying votes was and is an illegitimate form of political participation. I wonder if the use of political campaigning has crossed that line? I know that those who use lobbying funds have.

All that to remind you that whiteness has an agenda. Our history has defined normal America as white. Our family has not. White America was and is an illusion. As a Follower of Jesus, I can only reject the idea that the white American habits created in Virginia and applied throughout the country should be the norm. To the degree that has been true it is an aberration of the ideals commissioned by Jesus. I need to remind you that no human individual or community can perfectly meet the expectations of Jesus. This knowledge should be a basis for understanding and forgiveness not excuse making. I hope you have not read any place in this book where I have made excuses for our family or those who claim to follow Jesus for their commitment to the idolatry of whiteness.

For those of you who have made a commitment to be a Follower of

Jesus, you have established a life in which a framework greater than yourself is normative. If you have chosen not to be a Follower of Jesus, I regret that, but you need an alternative. Without such an outside presence you will have nothing to measure your living. Self-referential life is not nearly enough for either an individual or a nation. I suggest Jesus for either but let no one fool you. Our nation has never truly surrendered to his claims. At best we had the ideals contained in our founding documents. Those could have been enough, they were! Now we have abandoned any outside reference be it Jesus or our founding ideals. Today we are a self-referential people.

This sad development has given us President Trump. No American president has ever been more self-referential than him, but he is not the disease, he is the symptom. Loss of our ideals leads to the disease. Whiteness contributes. Greed contributes. False pride contributes. Each grows on the inability to see another reference point for evaluating things than some personal characteristic.

President Trump is an example of those who would destroy what they claim to honor or love if it means protecting or promoting themselves.

Take the controversy over athletes kneeling during the national anthem. It began as a protest to police involved shootings of black people, men in particular, who were unarmed. These shootings were interpreted as a continuation of oppression of blacks because they failed to fit the norm of whiteness. Because our society at large could not relate or would not relate to what they were protesting, the conversation became self-referential for many. It became about patriotism and honoring military sacrifice. Subverted in the process was the legitimate protest. Sadly, this is the pattern of legitimate protests, the voice spoken is delegitimized by changing the subject.

Empathy is a spiritual quality. I hope you are empathetic. Empathy is not compatible with being self-referential. Forgiveness is a spiritual quality. Living for others is a spiritual quality. Sacrifice is a spiritual quality. Being faithful (reliable) is a spiritual quality. Love is a spiritual quality. Do you remember these words?

> Love is patient; love is kind; love is not envious or boastful or arrogant or rude. It does not insist on its own way; it is not irritable or resentful; it does not rejoice in wrongdoing, but rejoices in the truth. It bears all things, believes all things, hopes all things, endures all things. Love never ends. I Corinthians 13: 4-8a. NRSV

If you follow Jesus you are compelled not only to express love for friends, but for your enemies as well. None of these spiritual qualities can be self-referential.

Grandma and I desire that you become people who live large lives. For those of you who are white we pray that you will find ways to surrender your social normalcy for the benefit of others. For those of you who are not white you will discover if you pay attention that there are ways that you can surrender personal advantage for the good of others, too.

These are the habits of justice.

Oh, by the way, you will not be perfect. Get over it. But try. Forgiveness is only fully possible for those who are not self-referential. To forgive is the definition of trading places with another and granting them what they need, a new start. We all fall down and we all need to get up. If you are standing when another falls, offer them a hand. It is the most likely the way one will be extended to you when you fall.

If all of this sounds like too much, hear this! It is more likely to happen if you stick together and change the family business from whiteness to justice. Also, remember it will take a life-time of work or at least it has for your grandparents.

We love you and pass on our flickering torch. Make it shine brighter.

Grandpa Jackson

REFERENCES

Allen, T.W. (1994). *The Invention of the white race* v. I. New York: Verso

Allen, T.W. (1994). *The Invention of the white race* v. II. New York: Verso

Bennett, L. (1972). *The Challenge of Blackness*. Chicago: Johnson
      Publishing Company

Buck, P.D., (2001). *Worked to the Bone: Race, Class, & Privilege in
      Kentucky*. New York: Monthly Review

Cone, J.H. (1975). *God of the Oppressed*. San Francisco: Harper

Davis, A, B.B. Gardner and M.R. Gardner. (1941). *Deep South: A Social
      Anthropological Study of Caste and Class*. Chicago: University of
      Chicago Press

Giddens, A. (1984). *The Constitution of society*. Berkley: University of
      California Press

Goodwin, D.K. (2005). *Team of Rivals: The Political Genius of Abraham
      Lincoln*. New York: Simon & Schuster

Hayes, C. (2012). Twilight of the Elites: America after Meritocracy. New
      York: Broadway Paperbacks

Martinot, S. (2003). *The rule of racialization: Class, identity, governance.*
      Philadelphia: Temple University Press

Mustard, D. <u>Racial, Ethnic, and Gender Disparities in Sentencing:
      Evidence from the U.S. Federal Courts</u>. Journal of Law and
      Economics, vol. XLIV (April 2001)

Myers, A.C. (1902). *Immigration of the Irish Quakers Into Pennsylvania*

1682-1750: with their early history in Ireland. Swathmore, PA.: The Author

Pettit, B. and B. Western. Mass Imprisonment and the Life Course: Race and Class Inequality in U.S. Incarceration. American Sociological Review, Vol. 69, No. 2 (Apr., 2004), pp. 151-169. American Sociological Association Stable URL: http://www.jstor.org/stable/3593082

Powell, J.A. (2012). *Racing to justice: Transforming our conceptions of self and other to build an inclusive society*. Bloomington: Indiana University Press

Sears, D., C. Van Laar, M. Carrillo, and R. Kosterman. Is it really Racism?: The origins of White Americas opposition to Race-targeted Policies. Public Opinion Quarterly, Vol. 61:16-53

Steffensmeier, D., J. Ulmer, and J. Kramer. The Interaction of Race, Gender, and Age in Criminal Sentencing: The Punishment Cost of Being Young, Black, and Male. Criminology, Vol 36, No.4 (1998) pp. 763-798

Weick, K.E. (1995). *Sensemaking in organizations*. Thousand Oaks: Sage

Western, B. and B. Pettit. Black-White Wage Inequality, Employment Rates, and Incarceration. American Journal of Sociology. Volume 111 Number 2 (September 2005): 553–78

Wink, W. (1984*). Naming the Powers*. Philadelphia: Fortress Press

ABOUT THE AUTHOR

Dwight Jackson has spent most of the last 40 years engaging communities at risk and advising / teaching those who would wish to work on behalf of these communities. He has working in, researched, wrote about, or taught about the issues facing US, African, and Asian urban and rural communities. Currently he is the CEO of the Sabbath Year Economic and Agriculture Development company which operates two model farms in Rwanda. He is on the board of the Rwandan NGO PROCOM which develops drinking water resources directly impacting the daily consumption of more than one million Rwandans. Recently he has returned to teaching part-time for Greenville University.

Also by Dr. Jackson
    Global Neighbors
    Sociologist Seeking Shalom